Yoga Kitchen

Recipes from the Shoshoni Yoga Retreat

Faith Stone and Rachael Guidry

Book Publishing Company
Summertown, Tennessee

Cover design: Warren Jefferson
Interior design: Gwynelle Dismukes
Photography: Faith Stone, Bob Carter, Tara Putorti
Line art: © 2003-2004 www.clipart.com

Book Publishing Company
P.O. Box 99
Summertown, TN 38483
1-888-260-8458

Printed in the United States
ISBN 1-57067-145-1
09   08   07   06   05   04   6   5   4   3   2   1

Stone, Faith, 1954-
    Yoga kitchen / Faith Stone & Rachael Guidry.
        p. cm.
    Includes index.
    ISBN 1-57067-145-1
    1. Vegetarian cookery. 2. Cookery, Yoga. I. Guidry,
Rachael. II. Title.

    TX837.S776 2004
    641.5'636--dc22

                        2004001909

Printed on recycled paper

The Book Publishing Co. is committed to preserving ancient forests and natural resources. We have elected to print this title on Torchglow Opaque, which is 30% postconsumer recycled and processed chlorine free. As a result of our paper choice, we have saved the following natural resources:

37.8 trees (40 feet in height)
11,025 gallons of water
6,458 kwh of electricity
94.5 pounds of air pollution

BOOK
PUBLISHING
COMPANY

We are a member of Green Press Initiative. For more information about Green Press Initiative visit: www.greenpressinitiative.org

We dedicate this book with love
and gratitude to our teacher,

Swami Shambhavananda Yogi.

contents

Specialties

Acknowledgements

Special thanks to Bob Carter of Blue Fusion Graphics. Bob has volunteered so much of his time and energy to help with the cookbook. We need to acknowledge Jo Stepaniak, our editor, for vastly improving our directions and making our measurements more precise. Her contributions make this a much better cookbook. We'd like to thank the Book Publishing Company and Cynthia and Bob Holzapfel in particular for their support and faith in our Yoga Kitchen at Shoshoni. We wish to thank all the wonderful folks who have visited Shoshoni, imbibed of our foods, participated in our yoga classes, and joined us in meditation. These wonderful souls inspire us to greater culinary heights, have expanded our hearts and vision, and have become our dear friends.

About the Authors

The Shoshoni kitchen is a melting pot of gastronomical inspiration. Our master chefs teach new yogis our yoga way of cooking and are always learning new recipes and ethnic dishes from them. Just as delicious soup improves by sitting just a bit longer, our Yoga Kitchen reverberates, marinates and assimilates the love and special talents of our ever-changing family of cooks. Holidays and festivals bring many friends, old and new, into the kitchen to bake pies, chop vegetables, blend sauces and dressings. Shanti and Faith have taught many Shoshoni chefs. We want to acknowledge all of the Shoshoni cooks past and present for contributing their love and creativity to the recipes in this book.

In 1994 Rachael (Shanti) Guidry came to study yoga and meditation with Shambhavananda. A native of Louisiana, she has always loved cooking for family and friends. For over eight years at Shoshoni she studied the art of gourmet vegetarian cuisine under the guidance of master chef Faith Stone. During that time, as kitchen manager and menu planner, Shanti led numerous cooking workshops. Her nourishing and delicious meals have inspired both visitors and residents of Shoshoni. Shanti still loves to cook at Shoshoni for special events and for her husband and daughter, Devika. Shanti currently is working on becoming certified as a Waldorf School teacher and pursuing a career in education.

Faith Stone has been studying yoga and meditation for over twenty-five years. She has lived in an ashram (community of yogis) since meeting Rudi, her spiritual teacher. She first practiced and then taught yoga and meditation to countless people who have passed through the ashram doors. Along with her yogi-husband, Shambhavananda Yogi, Faith is the codirector of Shoshoni Retreat and Eldorado Mountain Yoga Ashram. She is the coauthor of *The Shoshoni Cookbook*. For eighteen years, in order to support the ashram, Faith was the chef and owner of Rudi's Restaurant, a very successful vegetarian and natural foods eatery in Boulder, Colorado. Rudi's still is going strong under new owners. Faith won the Governor's Award for Excellence in Culinary Arts using native Colorado ingredients. She taught vegetarian and natural foods cooking classes to thousands of people throughout the state. Before owning the restaurant, Faith was an artist and returned to this venue in the form of traditional Tibetan thangka painting. Her thangkas are held in private collections, monasteries, and temples in the United States and India. Faith is a mom, one of her greatest joys, and has authored numerous articles on cooking, yoga, and parenting from a yogic perspective for national and local publications. She sings and plays ukulele.

Yoga Kitchen

Introduction

About Shoshoni

Shoshoni Yoga Retreat, named after nearby Shoshoni Mountain, rests on over two hundred acres of colorful Colorado high country surrounded by lush national forest. Our land has a friendly, joyful quality. Bright prayer flags and large Buddhas painted on rock walls adorn the valley much as one would see in India or Tibet. Log cabins nestled in the forest provide rustic charm with all the comforts of home for our guests.

A day at Shoshoni begins with morning meditation and chanting followed by a hearty, healthful breakfast. Our cuisine is low-fat, vegetarian, and very tasty. After a day of yoga, meditation, hiking, and healing Ayurvedic body treatments, guests often relax in the hot tub or doze on the deck overlooking nearby snow-capped peaks.

It is remarkable to watch the change in visitors as the Shoshoni environment strips away years of tightness and tension from their bodies and minds. Many guests attribute the change to the pristine mountain air, the pure spring water, and the incredible food. The resident yogis know it is the meditative energy (or shakti) that heals, cleanses, and restores people. And this energy is put into every dish prepared in the Shoshoni kitchen.

About Our Teacher

Shoshoni Yoga Retreat and Eldorado Mountain Yoga Ashram were founded by Shambhavananda Yogi. He is a radiant, big-hearted teacher who is a master of kundalini yoga. He teaches a method for meditation and growth called Shambhava yoga. His vision for Shoshoni and Eldorado is to create an environment conducive to inner growth that nurtures practitioners toward the realization of their true self, or Buddha nature. Facilities include residential areas for full-time yogis, nonresident classes, and retreat or visitor amenities.

Shambhavananda is rightly described by the name shambhav-ananda, which means the bliss of the natural state. His method of training students of yoga is unencumbered by dogma. He relates to the latent spiritual energy within aspirants, not to their limited view of themselves. Sri Nityananda, our root guru, taught, "The heart is the hub of all sacred places. Go there and roam in it." It is within this holy place that Shambhavananda encourages seekers to explore.

The Shoshoni Kitchen

The Shoshoni kitchen is a fascinating place. It was once a kitchen for a summer camp that served hundreds of children. Central to the kitchen is a new, shiny stove with two large ovens surrounded by giant stainless-steel pots, pans, cast-iron skillets, and hanging spoons and ladles. Five-gallon buckets overflow with various beans, grains, and colorful fresh vegetables. Quart jars brim with aromatic herbs and spices. Come on in and spend some time with our chefs.

Before daybreak, the breakfast cook enters the kitchen, lights the devotional candle, and puts on a chanting tape. The cook's quiet voice follows the chant as a large stainless-steel pot is hoisted onto the flame. In go the oats, water, and masala, and Indian cereal is started. Fresh muffins, toast, and fruit are prepared as the cook dances like a Shiva before dawn.

The Shoshoni staff works together to clean up after each meal. Guests love to join in the clean-up activities because a joyful family feeling makes work fun. After a brief morning meeting, the lunch cooks review the menu and plan for the day. Last-minute changes are almost always made to include the unexpected, such as the arrival of fresh-picked greens from the Eldorado Ashram. Today's lunch will be spanakopita, fragrant rice salad, and savory lentils. The chanting continues, creating a light atmosphere where the cooks focus on their work, repeating mantras as lunch is prepared.

Swamiji often enters the kitchen close to mealtime and tastes each dish. He takes a spoonful sample and a deep, inwardly focused breath. He immediately knows what it needs and, like a magician, transforms the food into nectar. The food is offered to Sri Nityananda, our root guru, and with a blessing chant it is served to a hungry group who just finished a hatha yoga class or chanting.

When we have a full house at Shoshoni, the kitchen is a hub of activity. Mountains of fresh vegetables are chopped with one-pointed perfection. We all wonder how we got it done. Somehow the shakti, or meditative energy, takes over and the results are delicious Shoshoni meals.

Shoshoni's two master cooks, Faith Stone and Rachael Guidry (Shanti), who created these delicious recipes, believe the most important ingredient in any dish is the heartfelt love put into it by the chefs.

Cooking with Shakti

People have been requesting our recipes for years. What makes the food so good? What did you put in this? How can vegetarian food taste so good? The cooks always look at each other and smile. They know that what is in the food can't be bought in the store or duplicated by the finest chefs. The magic ingredient we put into every dish is shakti—divine energy. Food is treated as divine sustenance because it contains the essence of life, a conscious energy that nourishes that same energy in you. The cook who seeks God in himself or herself while preparing food, cooks from a special place and adds shakti to the food.

Blessing the Food

Select a high, clean place in your kitchen where you can set up a small altar. Before serving your meal, offer the food to God with a prayer or blessing chant. At Shoshoni we prepare a plate of food for the lineage teachers. We offer it with a chant and then each item is stirred back into the original food. It is like adding a secret spice that turns the food into ambrosia.

Preparing to Cook

A very important element of cooking is the state you are in while preparing food. Anger, depression, or negativity can go into the food and give people a stomachache. No matter how you feel, pause a moment before you start and take a deep breath. Let go of thoughts just as you do in meditation, let go of negative emotions by breathing into your heart and allowing heavy tensions to drop down the arms and out of the hands. Shake the negative energy off your hands and repeat this exercise a few times while asking to release all deep negative tensions. Now, feel an openness in your heart and let that expand. Deep from within the heart a feeling of love wells up. Let that light energy flow down your arms and into your hands, which are your main tools for cooking. Feeling renewed, begin to cook with a clear mind and an open heart.

Mantra and Chanting in the Kitchen

Om Namah Shivayah, Om Namah Shivayah, Om Namah Shivayah, Om Namah Shivayah, Om Namah Shivayah, Om Namah Shivayah! Mantra repetition is the heartbeat of the kitchen. Mantra is sacred sound, infused with shakti (divine energy) and repeated silently or out loud to invoke that divine energy. Mantras permeate the cooks, permeate the food, and permeate you when you eat the food. If you have been given a mantra by your teacher, use that; if not, repeat "Om Namah Shivayah," which translates as "I bow with respect to my Inner Self," while preparing food.

Recipe for a Yogi

1 pound of insatiable desire to unite with God
365 days of practice
Handfuls of private retreats
Unlimited surrender
2 dashes of insanity
A sense of humor to taste

Combine all ingredients. Marinate in shakti.
Using one very good teacher to stir, bring to a boil,
and simmer for lifetimes. Serve with love and devotion.

Some Information About Ayurveda

Our cooking has been expanded to encompass the wonders of Ayurveda. This ancient Indian healing practice has changed our lives immeasurably. By following the principles of Ayurveda, we are bringing our bodies into balance so that we are uplifted in our spiritual practices. The result is a group of happy, healthy yogis. At the same time, we come from a tradition of spiritual teachers who relished the joy of eating a delicious meal. You will find that the recipes in this cookbook follow the middle path. We like to prepare tasty, healthy food following some basic Ayurvedic principles. Included is information about some of the recipes that may help you to know which are the best foods for your constitution and which season is the best time to eat certain foods. Following is a brief explanation of the three Ayurvedic doshas and more helpful hints about eating in harmony with the seasons.

Everyone is born with a certain set of physical, emotional, and mental characteristics. In Ayurveda this innate constitution is called *prakruti*. The five elements—earth, water, fire, air, and ether—come together to create your unique constitution. There are three groups of qualities or characteristics, called *doshas*:

Vata dosha is ruled by air and ether;
Pitta dosha is dominated by fire and water; and
Kapha dosha is ruled by water and earth.

The practice of Ayurveda is based on living in accordance with the rhythms of nature. An individual is not always in balance with his or her prakruti. To create balance you must know how to work with the nature of the imbalance. Food plays a big part in this process. Everything in nature has an energy or a combination of energies that can be observed through the five elements.

Vata dosha has the characteristics of being dry, light, cold, and rough. A predominantly Vata person may have a quick mind and lead an active life, always on the move. This is the nature of wind or air, which exemplifies the Vata dosha. A predominantly Pitta person has a fiery drive, a lot of creative energy, and a good digestive fire. Pittas tend to be leaders in whatever field they choose. A Kapha person is steady, calm, and grounded. Kaphas are blessed with the element of earth energy, which gives them a lot of endurance and stamina.

Although we all have each of the three doshas in our constitution, most people have a predominance of one or two doshas. Occasionally someone will have equal amounts of all three doshas.

Nature is like an intricately woven fabric. Unraveling one thread will affect the overall stability of the fabric. This analogy applies to the holistic system of Ayurveda. Understanding some basic principles and becoming aware of how our physical bodies move with the cycles of nature helps us keep up with the body's changing needs. Taking all the threads of the fabric into consideration keeps us balanced and in tune with nature's rhythms.

Eating in Harmony with the Seasons

Fall is a time of harvest, a time when the cold winds from the north start to blow and the leaves falling from the trees dry up and return to the earth. The plants become dormant, storing energy for the winter ahead. Vata dosha will be most out of balance in this season. Try to eat cooked foods prepared with warming spices—foods with sweet, sour, and salty tastes. Keep your body, especially your head, warm, and keep yourself lubricated inside and out by massaging your feet with warm sesame oil and using a little extra ghee in your food. Avoid foods that are drying or too spicy; avoid cold and raw foods; and avoid foods that are astringent or bitter in taste.

Winter is the season when we feel like curling up on the couch and hibernating. It is a predominantly Kapha season if winter where you live is damp and cold, or a Vata season if you live in a dry, cold, windy climate. Choose heavier foods to keep Vata balanced, such as whole grains, warming spices, hot soups and stews, beans, and hot teas. We often have a heartier appetite in the coldest months, because the digestive fire is stimulated by the contrasting cold weather. Everyone is aware of bulking up, especially around the holidays. However, storing too much weight may cause a Kapha imbalance.

Springtime is the season of rebirth. The snow begins to melt and the streams and rivers lose their icy coverings. The water begins to cleanse the earth. Kapha dosha will be most out of balance in this season. During the winter the body has stored and conserved energy. In spring we need to cleanse the excess and dry out a bit. Keep up your energy by staying active and avoiding foods that are too wet, oily, or sweet. Choose fresh vegetables over carbohydrates and choose foods with bitter, astringent, and pungent tastes.

Summer season is hot and sometimes humid in many areas. Pitta dosha will become aggravated in this season, so try to avoid getting overheated.

Keep as cool as you can internally and externally by avoiding hot spicy foods, oily foods, and stimulants such as caffeine. Focus on bitter, astringent, and sweet-tasting foods with an emphasis on fresh vegetables, fruits, and grains.

Along with having a specific taste or combination of tastes, every food has a corresponding energy. This energy falls into three categories, or *gunas*. *Sattwa* is the principle of light, peace, and purity. This sattvic principle works in conjunction with a yoga and meditation practice, helping one reach higher levels of consciousness. *Rajas* is the principle of movement, energy, and disturbance. Foods that have rajasic qualities will promote an active mind, making meditation difficult. *Tamas* has the qualities of darkness, dullness, and inactivity. A diet consisting mainly of tamasic foods will cause confusion, negativity, and dullness of mind.

Ayurveda is a system of health designed to work in conjunction with the pursuit of self-realization through the practices of yoga and meditation. By using these simple guidelines you can make choices in your diet that promote health and well-being while also supporting a dynamic spiritual practice.

Know your ingredients

Following is an introduction to the ingredients we commonly have on hand in our kitchen. Most of the ingredients can be found in your local grocery store or natural food store. If you have an Asian food market in your area, it will be a great resource for Indian and Asian food items.

Asafetida powder or hing: Asafetida is a commonly used Ayurvedic spice. It is a resin from the asafetida plant. Commonly called hing, asafetida has a flavor similar to garlic. Ayurvedic doctors say that it helps in digestion. It can be used as a substitute for onions or garlic in cooking. Yogis claim that hing is more sattvic than garlic and that it promotes mental peacefulness. It is particularly calming to Vata. Asafetida powder can be found in the bulk spice section of your natural food store or at an Indian market.

Bragg Liquid Aminos: This form of "soy sauce" is nutritionally superior to regular soy sauce because it contains sixteen amino acids. It also is easier to digest, especially for those who are wheat-sensitive or who are avoiding fermented foods. We use it to flavor soups, sauces, and any kind of vegetable or grain dish.

Chickpea flour or besan flour: This is a flour made from ground, raw chickpeas and is a commonly used ingredient in Indian recipes. It is available at Indian markets, Asian food markets, or even in bulk at a natural food store.

Dal: In India, dal refers to a pea or bean soup, though in translation the word means "split." However, the name also is used in Indian cooking for a finished lentil or bean dish, even when the beans are left whole. There are several dal recipes in this book that call for split and skinned mung beans, split urad dal, or toor dal. Mung dal in particular can be made with whole green mung beans, split mung beans with the skins still on, and split mung beans with the skins removed. The latter is referred to as "golden mung dal." They all have a slightly different taste and texture. These varieties can be found in Indian and Asian food stores, where they typically carry a wide variety of beans and peas commonly used in Indian and Ayurvedic cooking.

Fenugreek leaves: Dried fenugreek leaves are available in Indian groceries. They lend a unique savory and distinctively Indian flavor to a dish. If unavailable, we generally substitute fresh or dried basil leaves. Although not quite the same taste, they still are delicious.

Flaxseeds: If you are vegan and wonder what to substitute for eggs in your baking recipes, flaxseeds work very well and they add extra nutrition to your dish. Flaxseeds can be found packaged or in bulk in the health food section of your grocery store or in your natural food market.

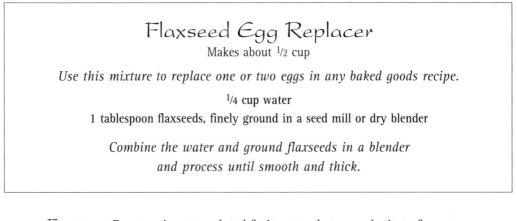

Flaxseed Egg Replacer
Makes about ½ cup

Use this mixture to replace one or two eggs in any baked goods recipe.

¼ cup water
1 tablespoon flaxseeds, finely ground in a seed mill or dry blender

*Combine the water and ground flaxseeds in a blender
and process until smooth and thick.*

Fructose: Fructose is a granulated fruit sugar that we substitute for regular white sugar in recipes where a lighter-colored pastry, pudding, or sauce is desired.

Ghee: Ghee is butter cooked until it is completely clarified—that is, when all of the milk solids have separated from the clear butterfat. It is easily made by gently simmering butter (preferably organic) until the milk solids separate from the fat. The use of ghee in cooking greatly enhances the body's ability to absorb nutrients. It is especially building and nourishing for Vata dosha.

Japanese eggplant: This is a long, thin, light purple vegetable that has a pleasant, mild flavor. It is commonly found in most grocery stores or in Indian and Asian markets.

Louki squash: This is a zucchini-like vegetable found in Indian and Asian markets. It has a light, cooling taste that is perfect for use in summer curries. For a similar taste, regular zucchini squash can be substituted in any recipe calling for louki.

Natural sugar: Natural sugar includes Sucanat (see below), which can be used for darker baked goods and sauces, and granulated fructose, which can be used for light-colored baked goods and sauces. At times you may also use pure maple syrup.

Panir cheese: This quick and easy homemade cheese makes any curry dish special. It is made by boiling whole milk and separating it into curds and whey with the addition of lime juice or a little vinegar. The curds are then strained through cheesecloth and allowed to harden into a simple cheese. Cut the cheese into chunks and then pan-fry it until it is browned. Panir adds flavor and protein to a meal. (See Curried Zucchini and Bell Peppers, page 106, for a recipe that uses panir.)

Rice noodles and rice paper wraps: Rice noodles often are available in the Asian section of most regular supermarkets. Rice paper wraps are available in Asian markets and come in an array of sizes and varieties.

Sea Salt: We always prefer to use natural sea salt instead of common table salt. Sea salt contains vital minerals without the added chemicals typically found in table salt.

Sucanat: Sucanat is a trademark name for evaporated cane juice crystals combined with blackstrap molasses. We use it as one of our main sweeteners because it has more to offer us nutritionally than other refined sugars. Sucanat contains more complex carbohydrates, so the body takes longer to assimilate it. Thus we avoid the "sugar high" and crash of most overly refined, denatured sweeteners. Sucanat will impart a rich flavor and a deep, dark color to your pastries. If you want a lighter result, use granulated fructose or natural cane sugar.

Toasted nori sheets: Also called sushi nori, these flat sheets of seaweed are used to make sushi rolls. They are found in the Asian section of most supermarkets or in Asian grocery stores.

Wasabi: This pale green horseradish is served as a condiment with sushi nori rolls. It is available prepared or powdered in the Asian section of most supermarkets, in Asian markets, and in many natural food stores.

Yoga Kitchen

Recipes

Appetizers

Asparagus Koftas   18

Butternut Squash and Roasted Garlic Spread   19

Baked Corn and Coconut Kachoris   20

Feta Rolled Eggplant   21

Fried Sweet Potato Chips   22

Homemade Urad Dal Patties   22

Tofu Sunflower Seed Meatballs   23

Millet Croquettes   24

Mung Bean Hummus 25

Roasted Vegetable Quesadillas   26

Sesame and Spinach Dal Badis   27

Thai Spring Rolls with Spicy Fresh Basil   28

Asparagus Koftas

Koftas are made from any combination of chopped vegetables and spices mixed with chickpea flour to form a batter then fried until crispy and golden. You can start with this recipe, but the possibilities are endless. Try substituting cabbage, cauliflower, sweet potatoes, and summer squashes for the asparagus. Curry Cottage Cheese Sauce, page 59, is an excellent accompaniment.

Combine all of the ingredients in a large bowl, adding a little water if needed to hold the batter together.

3 cups finely chopped fresh asparagus

1 cup chickpea flour

3 tablespoons minced fresh cilantro

1 tablespoon minced fresh ginger

2 teaspoons salt

1/2 teaspoon turmeric

1/2 teaspoon Garam Masala, page 70

1/2 teaspoon baking powder

Oil for frying

Heat about one inch of oil in a heavy-bottomed skillet. Drop the batter by the tablespoonful into the hot oil and fry for about 5 minutes or until the koftas turn golden brown. Remove with a slotted spoon and drain well on a paper towel.

Butternut Squash and Roasted Garlic Spread

Serves 6

The taste of roasted garlic is undeniably rich and warming. Serve this dip on the side with Mediterranean Red Lentil and Spinach Stew with Currants, page 91, warm pita bread, and Fresh Herb and Baby Greens Salad, page 30. This dish is always a favorite of our guests.

Place water in a saucepan and bring to a boil. Add the squash and cook uncovered for about 20 minutes or until tender. Drain well.

4 cups water

2 cups peeled and cubed butternut, acorn, or pumpkin squash

3 tablespoons roasted nut or seed butter (such as tahini, almond butter, or cashew butter)

4 cloves roasted garlic *(see note)*

1 tablespoon fresh lemon juice

1 teaspoon salt

1 teaspoon ground coriander

1/4 cup finely chopped fresh parsley

Transfer the squash to a food processor along with the nut butter, roasted garlic, lemon juice, salt, and coriander. Blend until smooth. Add the parsley and pulse a few times to mix.

Note: We roast several whole heads of garlic at a time in a 350°F oven for about 30 minutes. Let the garlic cool a little. Press the cloves and the pulp will squeeze out from the skins. Roasted garlic is delicious just as it is on bread and can be added to soups and vegetable dishes. It keeps in the refrigerator for about a week in a tightly sealed jar.

Baked Corn and Coconut Kachoris

Every Sunday at Shoshoni we serve a delicious Indian feast. The cooks never can make enough of these little delicacies. They are especially delicious served with Fresh Ginger and Date Chutney, page 55, and Coriander Spiced Yogurt, page 60.

1 3/4 cups whole wheat pastry flour

1/4 cup cornmeal

1 teaspoon salt

1/4 teaspoon natural sugar

4 tablespoons cold ghee or
   unsalted butter

7 tablespoons ice water

1 1/2 cups cooked fresh or frozen
   corn kernels

3 tablespoons grated dried coconut

1 teaspoon salt

1 teaspoon ground coriander

1 teaspoon minced fresh ginger

1/2 teaspoon Garam Masala, page 70

1/4 teaspoon cayenne pepper

Combine the flour, cornmeal, salt, and sugar in a medium bowl. Cut in the ghee using a pastry cutter or two forks, and then work it into the flour using your fingertips. Add the water and mix to form a ball of dough. Knead on a lightly floured surface for 2 to 3 minutes until the dough is smooth and pliable.

Place the corn, coconut, salt, coriander, fresh ginger, Garam Masala, and cayenne pepper in a food processor and pulse 3 or 4 times to blend.

Preheat the oven to 375°F. Liberally oil a baking sheet.

Divide the dough in half. On a floured surface, roll each piece into a log. Slice each log into about 18 small pieces. Roll each piece of dough out into a 3- or 4-inch circle. Place 1 tablespoon of filling in the center and fold the circle in half. With the tines of a fork press all around the edge of the pastry to seal it fully. Place the pastries on the prepared baking sheet.

Brush each pastry with a little melted ghee, coating it thoroughly. Bake for 25 to 30 minutes or until the kachoris are golden brown.

Feta Rolled Eggplant

Serves 6

Faith loves eggplant! She created this simple dish combining the mellow taste of pan-fried eggplant and the pungent contrast of feta cheese. This dish is influenced by a passion for Greek and Middle Eastern food. It's delicious served with Bulgur Pilaf, page 167, and a fresh green salad with Moroccan Vinaigrette, page 50.

1 large eggplant

Salt as needed

6 ounces feta cheese

1 cup unbleached white or whole wheat flour

1 tablespoon dried basil

1/2 teaspoon salt

Pinch of pepper

Olive oil for pan-frying

Peel the eggplant and slice it lengthwise into 1/4-inch pieces. Lightly salt the slices of eggplant and press them between paper towels. You do not need to put a weight on top. The salt causes the eggplant slices to sweat and removes excess moisture and bitterness. Let the slices sit for 15 minutes and then wipe off the salt and moisture.

Combine the flour with the basil, 1/2 teaspoon salt, and a pinch of pepper. Dredge the eggplant slices in the seasoned flour. Heat 1/8 inch of olive oil in a cast-iron skillet or sauté pan. Fry the eggplant slices until tender and browned on both sides.

Slice the feta cheese into sticks. Place 1 stick on each of the sautéed eggplant slices and roll the eggplant around it. Serve warm or chilled.

Fried Sweet Potato Chips

These tasty chips are sure to be a hit with kids. Also try them as a garnish for Vietnamese Vegetable Rice Noodle Bowl, page 96, or Udon Noodles with Grilled Tofu and Mandarin Sauce, page 124.

2 cups canola or sunflower oil

1 large sweet potato, peeled and sliced very thinly

Salt

Heat the oil in a heavy-bottomed pot and fry the sweet potatoes in it until golden brown. Drain well on paper towels. Sprinkle lightly with salt to taste, if desired.

Homemade Urad Dal Patties

These light, delicious, pan-fried patties can be served as an accompaniment to an Indian feast along with Cucumber Mint Raita, page 60, and Fresh Coconut and Green Chili Chutney, page 54.

1 cup split urad dal

2 tablespoons minced onion

1/2 teaspoon salt

1/2 teaspoon turmeric

3 tablespoons canola oil

Soak the urad dal in 3 cups of water for 2 hours or overnight. Rinse and drain the dal in a mesh colander. Place the dal and 1/2 cup of fresh water in a food processor and blend into a smooth paste. Transfer to a bowl, cover, and set in a warm place to ferment for 1 to 2 hours.

Fold the onion, salt, and turmeric into the batter, mixing well. Heat the oil in a cast-iron skillet. Using a tablespoon, scoop up some batter and drop it into the skillet. Flatten the patty with the back of a spatula. Sauté each patty on both sides until browned and cooked in the center. Drain on a paper towel to absorb any excess oil.

Tofu Sunflower Seed Meatballs

Serves 6

These little meatballs are a hit as an appetizer dipped in Savory Red Sauce, page 109, or as an addition to Spinach Fettuccine with Almond Basil Sauce, page 118.

Preheat the oven to 375°F. Oil a 9 x 13-inch baking dish.

Grind the sunflower seeds in a food processor, remove, and set aside. Place half the tofu in the food processor and blend until creamy and smooth. Crumble the remaining half of the tofu into a bowl. Add the ground sunflower seeds, creamed tofu, bread crumbs, and flour. Mix briefly, then stir in the soy sauce, herbs, salt, and pepper. Stir to blend well.

1 pound firm tofu, well drained

1/2 cup toasted sunflower seeds

1/2 cup coarse dried bread crumbs

2 tablespoons chickpea flour or barley flour

3 tablespoons Bragg Liquid Aminos or natural soy sauce

1 tablespoon fresh dill, minced, or 1 teaspoon dried dill

1 tablespoon minced fresh sage, or 1 teaspoon dried sage

1 1/2 teaspoons minced fresh rosemary, or 1/2 teaspoon dried rosemary

1 teaspoon salt

1/4 teaspoon pepper

Put a little oil on your hands and form small balls with the batter. Place them into the prepared baking dish. Bake for 20 to 30 minutes or until well browned and a little crispy. For the best results as an appetizer, serve hot out of the oven.

Millet Croquettes

These little delicacies are a lovely accompaniment to a light vegetable soup. You can also serve them in a warm pita pocket with Coriander Spiced Yogurt, page 60.

1 cup millet

2³/4 cups boiling water

¹/2 teaspoon salt

¹/3 cup grated carrots

3 tablespoons chickpea flour

3 tablespoons sunflower seeds

3 tablespoons Bragg Liquid Aminos
   or natural soy sauce

3 tablespoons minced fresh parsley

³/4 teaspoon ground cumin

¹/2 teaspoon ground coriander

Generous pinch of pepper

Oil for frying

Dry-roast the millet in a saucepan, stirring constantly until it begins to smell like popcorn and turns golden brown. Turn off the heat and add the boiling water and the salt. Cover the pan and bring to a boil. Reduce the heat to medium and cook 20 to 25 minutes.

Transfer the cooked millet to a bowl and stir in the carrots, chickpea flour, sunflower seeds, Bragg Liquid Aminos, parsley, cumin, coriander, and pepper. Heat about 1 inch of oil in a heavy-bottomed skillet. Form tablespoon-size balls of the millet mixture and drop them into the hot oil. Fry 5 minutes or until golden brown. Remove the croquettes with a slotted spoon and drain well on a paper towel. They are best served hot.

Note: You may bake these croquettes instead of frying them. Simply preheat the oven to 375°F and coat a baking pan with olive oil. Put a little oil on your hands and roll the balls between your palms to coat them with oil. Bake uncovered for 20 minutes or until browned on the outside.

Mung Bean Hummus

Hummus is a great high-protein addition to any meal. Serve it as an appetizer with crisp crackers or warmed pita bread or as a spread for your favorite sandwich. This hummus, which is made from mung beans, is easier to digest than its traditional counterpart.

Combine the vegetable stock with the mung dal in a large pot. Bring to a boil, lower the heat to medium-high, and simmer until tender. This will take about 1 hour. Drain the dal and reserve 1/4 cup of the liquid to blend with the hummus.

Transfer the drained dal and reserved liquid to a food processor along with the tahini, lemon juice, olive oil, salt, garlic, cumin, coriander, and optional Tabasco. Process until smooth. Add the cilantro and pulse a few times to blend.

4 cups of vegetable stock or water

1 1/2 cups golden mung dal

3 tablespoons sesame tahini

Juice of 1 lemon (about 3 tablespoons)

2 tablespoons olive oil or ghee, melted

2 teaspoons salt

1 clove garlic

1 teaspoon ground cumin

1 teaspoon ground coriander

Dash of Tabasco (optional)

1/2 cup chopped fresh cilantro

Roasted Vegetable Quesadillas

These dairy-free quesadillas are stuffed with tofu and spiced vegetables. Serve them as a starter to a Mexican feast or have them as a main dish accompanied by Zesty Mango Salsa, page 64.

1 whole red bell pepper

3 tablespoons olive oil

2 cloves garlic, minced

12 ounces firm tofu

1/4 cup minced fresh cilantro

3 tablespoons fresh lime juice

2 tablespoons Bragg Liquid Aminos or natural soy sauce

1 teaspoon ground coriander

1 teaspoon ground cumin

Salt and pepper

1 tablespoon olive oil

1/2 onion, thinly sliced

1 zucchini, very thinly sliced

8 whole wheat tortillas

Using a gas stove or grill, roast the red pepper over an open flame until blackened on the outside. Remove the charred skin, stem, and seeds and set the pepper aside. For those using an electric range, roast the peppers on a baking sheet in a preheated 500°F oven for 20 minutes or until blackened all over.

Heat 2 tablespoons of the olive oil in a skillet. Add the garlic and sauté until brown. Place the pepper, garlic, tofu, cilantro, lime juice, Bragg Liquid Aminos, coriander, cumin, and salt and pepper to taste in a food processor and blend into a smooth paste.

Heat the remaining 1 tablespoon of oil in the skillet until very hot. Add the onion and quickly sauté over high heat until it begins to brown. Add the zucchini and continue to sauté until browned and soft.

Spread 1/4 of the roasted pepper paste over a tortilla and add 1/4 of the onion and squash mixture. Lay another tortilla over the top. This makes one quesadilla. Continue until all of the quesadillas are made. Heat the skillet again and toast each quesadilla until lightly browned on each side. Cut them into quarters and arrange them on a serving plate with fresh salsa and guacamole.

Sesame and Spinach Dal Badis

The flavors of these crispy fried fritters blend wonderfully to make a delicious high-protein appetizer or accompaniment to an Indian feast. Serve them with Cucumber Mint Raita, page 60, and Sweet Fennel and Tomato Chutney, page 58.

Rinse and drain the dal. Place the dal, water, ginger, and chili in a food processor and blend into a smooth batter.

½ cup split mung beans, soaked overnight

2 tablespoons water

1 teaspoon minced fresh ginger

½ hot green chili, seeded and minced

3 cups (about 12 ounces) fresh spinach, chopped

¼ cup chickpea flour

3 tablespoons white sesame seeds

2 teaspoons salt

1 teaspoon ground coriander

½ teaspoon turmeric

½ teaspoon baking powder

¼ teaspoon grated nutmeg

Vegetable oil for frying

Place the spinach in a dry skillet and briefly sauté until wilted. Drain off all the liquid. Stir the cooked spinach and the remaining ingredients into the batter. Mix well.

Place about 1 inch of oil in a heavy iron skillet or heavy-bottomed saucepan and heat until hot but not smoking. Scoop about 1 tablespoon of batter per badi and drop it into the oil. You can cook about 12 badis at the same time. Remove them from the oil with a slotted spoon when they have browned and drain them on paper towels. Continue to cook until all of the batter has been used. Badis are best served immediately, but they will also keep hot and fresh for up to an hour in a warm oven.

Thai Spring Rolls with Spicy Fresh Basil

Thai food is always a favorite. These fresh spring rolls are the perfect start for a Thai feast including Thai Vegetable Curry, page 94. Serve them with Roasted Peanut Dipping Sauce, page 65, on the side.

Slice the block of tofu lengthwise into 1-inch-thick pieces or squares. Heat the sesame oil in a skillet and fry the tofu pieces until golden and crisp on all sides. Pour the soy sauce over the tofu and flip it to coat both sides. Remove the tofu and transfer it to a cutting board. Cut into long thin strips and set aside.

Combine the lettuce, carrots, bean sprouts, rice vermicelli, cucumber, basil, cilantro, lime juice, sugar, jalapeño, and ginger in a bowl and toss lightly to mix. Soak several pieces of rice paper at a time in warm water until soft. Remove the papers from the water and place them flat on a clean towel. Place 1/4 to 1/3 cup of the vegetable mixture in the center of the rice paper. Lay a few pieces of tofu over the top. Fold the wrap and filling in half, gently squeezing the ingredients into as tight a roll as possible without tearing the rice paper. Fold in the sides, roll the rest of the way, and chill. Slice the rolls in half before serving.

4 ounces firm tofu

1 tablespoon toasted sesame oil

3 tablespoons natural soy sauce

2 cups shredded green leaf lettuce

1 cup shredded carrots

1 cup mung bean sprouts

2 ounces rice vermicelli, soaked until soft and drained

1/2 cucumber, peeled, seeded, and thinly sliced lengthwise into 3-inch lengths

1/2 cup coarsely chopped fresh Thai basil or regular basil

1/4 cup chopped fresh cilantro

1/4 cup fresh lime juice

2 tablespoons natural sugar

1 tablespoon minced jalapeño pepper

1 tablespoon minced fresh ginger

12 sheets small rice paper wraps

Salads

Fresh Herb and Baby Greens Salad

Serves 4

Fresh herbs and organic greens are abundant in summer, taking over our garden at Eldorado Springs Ashram. This crisp, easy salad will complement any main dish or soup beautifully.

Combine the lettuce, greens, cucumber, basil, cilantro, dill, and rosemary in a large salad bowl and toss gently. Garnish each plate of salad with a little of the grated carrots and beets or use them to garnish the whole salad if served in the bowl.

1 head butter lettuce or other tender, flavorful variety

1 generous handful of mixed baby greens

1 cup peeled, seeded, and thinly sliced cucumber

1/4 cup fresh basil leaves

1/4 cup fresh cilantro leaves

2 tablespoons coarsely chopped fresh dill

1 tablespoon coarsely chopped fresh rosemary

1/2 cup grated carrots

1/2 cup grated raw beets

Marinated Asparagus Primavera Salad

You are sure to enjoy this elegant, tasty springtime salad.

1 pound fresh asparagus

1/2 cup yellow and red bell pepper strips (about 1/2 pepper of each color)

1/2 cup light olive oil or sunflower oil

1/4 cup fresh lemon juice or raspberry vinegar

1 tablespoon apple juice concentrate

1/2 teaspoon salt

1/2 teaspoon pepper

1 clove garlic, minced

1/2 cup minced fresh basil

Snap off and discard the tough ends of the asparagus and steam the stalks whole. When almost tender, add the bell pepper strips and steam lightly. Remove from the heat, drain, and transfer to a bowl.

Combine the oil, lemon juice, apple juice concentrate, salt, pepper, and garlic in a blender and process until well blended. Stir in the fresh basil and pour over the vegetables. Serve warm or chill for a few hours for a cold salad in summer.

Pasta Salad with Basil Pesto

Serves 4

In summer the Eldorado Springs Ashram garden is overflowing with different varieties of fresh basil. Pesto and pasta dishes are the perfect way to take advantage of this wonderfully fragrant, delicious herb.

Combine all the pesto ingredients in a food processor and grind into a thick paste. The pesto will keep one week in the refrigerator or several weeks in the freezer.

Combine the salad ingredients in a large bowl. Toss with sufficient pesto to suit your taste.

Pesto

2 cups fresh basil leaves

1/2 cup extra-virgin olive oil

1/2 cup walnuts

1/4 cup freshly grated Parmesan cheese

2 large cloves garlic

1/2 teaspoon salt

1/4 teaspoon pepper

Pasta Salad

6 ounces unusually shaped pasta (spirals, shells, wheels, or others), cooked al dente and drained

1/2 head of romaine or Bibb lettuce, torn into bite-size pieces

2 large tomatoes, cut into wedges

1/2 bunch of scallions, minced (about 1/2 cup)

3 tablespoons extra-virgin olive oil

3 tablespoons apple cider vinegar

Sesame Snow Pea Salad

This salad of crunchy, fresh Asian vegetables makes a beautiful side dish to Stir Fried Rice with Whole Cashews, page 173, or Vietnamese Vegetable Rice Noodle Bowl, page 96.

Snap off the tough ends and string the snow peas. Very lightly steam the snow peas, cabbage, radish, carrots, and bell pepper so they still have a nice crunch and retain their bright colors. Place all the vegetables in a bowl and toss gently to cool.

Combine the soy sauce, apple juice, sesame seeds, sesame oil, honey, and anise in a separate bowl. Pour over the vegetables. Add the mung bean sprouts and toss gently. Serve warm in winter or chilled in summer. Garnish with the fresh cilantro just before serving.

2 cups fresh snow peas

1/2 cup shredded purple cabbage

1/4 cup julienned daikon radish

1/4 cup julienned carrots

1/4 cup thinly sliced red bell pepper

1/4 cup natural soy sauce

1/4 cup apple juice

3 tablespoons sesame seeds

2 tablespoons toasted sesame oil

1 tablespoon honey

1 teaspoon ground anise

1/2 cup mung bean sprouts

1/4 cup chopped fresh cilantro

Southwestern Barley Salad

Here is a refreshingly different way to serve barley. It makes a hearty and flavorful side dish served warm in winter or room temperature in summer.

Place 2½ cups of the water, the barley, and 1 teaspoon salt in a medium saucepan and bring to a boil. Cover and simmer over medium heat for 45 to 50 minutes or until the barley has absorbed the water and is tender.

Place the remaining 1 cup of water in a separate saucepan and bring to a boil. Add the corn and cook uncovered for about 10 minutes or until tender. Drain well.

Meanwhile, combine the bell peppers, optional tomatillos, pine nuts, onions, scallions, celery, sage, salt to taste, and pepper in a large bowl. When the barley is done, place it in a mesh colander and rinse to remove the excess gluten. Drain well and add to the salad vegetables along with the cooked corn.

Barley Salad

3½ cups water

1 cup pearl barley

1 teaspoon salt

½ cup fresh or frozen corn kernels

½ cup diced red bell pepper

½ cup diced yellow pepper

½ cup toasted pine nuts

3 tomatillos, chopped (optional)

¼ cup finely chopped purple onions

¼ cup chopped scallions

1 stalk celery, diced

3 tablespoons minced fresh sage or summer savory, or 2 teaspoons dried sage or savory

1 to 2 teaspoons salt

¼ teaspoon pepper

Chipotle Chili Dressing

1 cup minced fresh cilantro

1/4 cup corn oil

1/4 cup fresh lime juice

1/2 to 1 tablespoon
   minced chipotle chilies

Salt

To prepare the dressing, place 1/2 cup of the cilantro and the oil, lime juice, chilies, and salt to taste in a blender. Process until well combined. Pour the dressing over the barley and vegetables, add the remaining 1/2 cup cilantro, and mix well. Serve at room temperature or lightly chilled.

Tempeh Salad with Homemade Soy Mayonnaise

Serves 4

This simple salad makes a high-protein side dish served on whole grain crackers. It also makes a delicious sandwich served in pita pockets or on whole grain bread.

Heat the oil in a large skillet. Add the tempeh and fry until golden. Sprinkle the Bragg Liquid Aminos over the tempeh and sauté for 1 minute longer. Transfer to a serving bowl and stir in the mayonnaise, scallions, bell peppers, carrots, celery, parsley, and salt and pepper to taste. Mix thoroughly. Let marinate in the refrigerator for 1 hour before serving. Use more or less mayonnaise depending on your taste.

2 tablespoons sunflower oil

4 cups cubed tempeh

3 tablespoons Bragg Liquid Aminos

1 to 2 cups Homemade Soy
   Mayonnaise, page 63, or
   prepared mayonnaise

1/2 cup chopped scallions

1/2 cup diced red bell peppers

1/2 cup diced carrots

1/4 cup diced celery

1/4 cup minced fresh parsley

Salt and pepper

Thai Rice Noodle and Peanut Salad

This traditional Thai salad is delicious served along with Thai Spring Rolls with Spicy Fresh Basil, page 28, or Coconut Curry Calzones, page 184.

Soak the noodles in warm water for 10 minutes or boil them until al dente, about 3 minutes. Rinse thoroughly with cold water, drain, and place in a serving bowl with the bean sprouts, carrots, bell peppers, and peas.

Combine the coconut milk, peanut butter, honey, ginger, salt, lemon juice, optional curry paste, and turmeric in a blender and process until smooth. Pour over the noodles and toss to mix well. Allow the salad to marinate in the refrigerator for about 1 hour. Garnish with the peanuts, basil, and lemon zest just before serving.

1 (8-ounce) package fine rice noodles

1 cup mung bean sprouts

1/2 cup finely julienned carrots

1/2 cup thinly sliced red bell peppers

1/2 cup fresh green peas, steamed for 3 minutes, or thawed frozen peas

1/2 cup coconut milk

1/4 cup natural peanut butter

2 tablespoons honey

1 tablespoon minced fresh ginger

2 teaspoons salt

2 teaspoons fresh lemon juice

1 teaspoon Thai red curry paste (optional)

1/2 teaspoon turmeric

1/2 cup roasted peanuts, coarsely chopped

1/4 cup coarsely chopped fresh Thai basil or regular basil

1 tablespoon lemon zest

Toasted Millet Tabouli Salad

Millet is often overlooked. It is packed with more nutrition and flavor than bulgur wheat, which is the grain most frequently used in tabouli.

1 tablespoon ghee

2 cups millet, rinsed and drained well

3 1/2 cups boiling water

1/2 cup bite-size cauliflower florets

1/2 cup finely chopped red bell peppers

1/4 cup finely chopped carrots

1 bunch of fresh parsley, minced

1 cup finely chopped raw spinach

1/4 cup sunflower oil

1/4 cup currants or finely chopped dates

1/4 cup minced fresh mint

1/4 cup thinly sliced scallions

3 tablespoons fresh lemon juice

1 tablespoon Bragg Liquid Aminos
   or natural soy sauce

1 tablespoon orange juice

2 teaspoons ground coriander

1 to 2 teaspoons salt

1/2 teaspoon ground cumin

1 clove garlic, minced

Pinch of pepper

Heat the ghee in a heavy-bottomed pan. Add the millet and toast it until the grains are nicely browned and emit a nutty aroma. Carefully add the boiling water, cover, and simmer over low heat for 20 to 30 minutes. When tender, transfer to a bowl to cool, and fluff the grains with a fork.

While the millet is cooking, lightly steam the cauliflower, bell peppers, and carrots. To make the dressing, combine the parsley, spinach, oil, currants, mint, scallions, lemon juice, Bragg Liquid Aminos, orange juice, coriander, salt, cumin, garlic, and pepper in a medium bowl. Pour over the millet. Add the steamed vegetables and mix well. Serve chilled in the summer or at room temperature in the colder months.

Tossed Greens and Strawberry Salad

Serves 4

The flavors of fresh garden greens, strawberries, and almonds combine to make a beautiful, tasty salad.

Assemble the salad just before serving. Toss the greens with olive oil to coat the leaves lightly. Add the vinegar, freshly ground pepper, and a dash of hot sauce and gently toss again. Arrange on chilled plates, garnish with the sliced strawberry halves and optional raw almonds.

6 cups fresh organic greens (may include edible flowers), rinsed and spun or patted dry

6 tablespoons olive oil

3 tablespoons balsamic or rice vinegar

1 teaspoon fresh peppercorns (black or other variety), ground

Dash of your favorite hot sauce

1 pint fresh strawberries (preferably organic), sliced in half

1/2 cup whole raw almonds with skins (optional)

Tropical Fruit and Nut Salad

This special-occasion fruit salad is beautiful and rich with the tastes of the tropics. Serve this salad as a light and colorful brunch dish on its own or for a weekend breakfast treat during the summer months.

1 cup diced red apple

1 cup sliced bananas

1/4 cup fresh lemon juice

1 cup diced pineapple

1/2 cup peeled and diced mango

1/2 cup kiwi, peeled and sliced into half-moons

1/4 cup shredded coconut

1/4 cup slivered almonds, cashews, or macadamia nuts

1/4 cup pitted and sliced dates or sliced fresh figs

1/2 cup plain or lemon yogurt

1 tablespoon honey

1/4 cup fresh mint leaves

Place the apples and bananas in a medium bowl and toss them with the lemon juice. Add the pineapple, mango, kiwi, coconut, almonds, and dates, and mix gently.

Combine the yogurt and honey and stir until well blended. Pour over the fruit, folding it in gently. Garnish with the fresh mint leaves.

Trés Colores Vegetable Salad

This simple and nutritious salad is so colorful it brightens up any simple meal. In summer you can find many varieties of cherry tomatoes. Try using yellow and orange cherry tomatoes to make this salad extra special.

1 cup peeled sweet potato chunks

2 cups broccoli florets, lightly steamed

1 cup cherry tomatoes, sliced in half

1/2 yellow bell pepper, thinly sliced

1/4 cup sunflower oil

1/4 cup minced fresh dill

Juice of 1 lemon (about 3 tablespoons)

2 tablespoons honey

1 tablespoon Dijon or stone-ground mustard

1 teaspoon salt

1/4 teaspoon pepper

Boil the sweet potatoes in water until tender but firm, about 20 minutes. Combine the sweet potatoes, broccoli, cherry tomatoes, and bell peppers in a salad bowl. In a separate bowl, whisk together the oil, dill, lemon juice, honey, mustard, salt, and pepper and pour over the vegetables. Toss gently. Let the salad marinate in the refrigerator for 1 hour before serving.

Vegetarian Caesar Salad

This is another of our most popular salads. At the end of the meal the bowl is always empty. The salad goes well with almost any dish from simple soups to an Italian feast.

1 head romaine lettuce

2 tablespoons olive oil

2 cloves garlic, minced

1 package (about 12 ounces) extra-firm silken tofu

1/4 cup water

3 tablespoons fresh lemon juice

1 tablespoon honey

2 teaspoons salt

1 teaspoon dried dill

1/2 cup coarsely chopped fresh parsley

1/2 cup sun-dried tomatoes, soaked, drained, and finely chopped

1/2 cup croutons

1/4 cup freshly grated Parmesan cheese (optional)

Wash the lettuce in very cold water and spin dry. Carefully tear the leaves into bite-size pieces and arrange them in a salad bowl. Place in the refrigerator until you are ready to serve the salad.

Heat the olive oil in a skillet and roast the garlic until browned. Transfer to a blender along with the tofu, water, lemon juice, honey, salt, and dill. Process until creamy. Add the parsley and pulse a few times to mix it in. Pour the dressing over the romaine, tossing to coat the lettuce thoroughly. Add the sun-dried tomatoes and croutons and toss again. Sprinkle with the optional Parmesan cheese just before serving. Serve at once.

Wilted Spinach and Tofu Feta Salad

Serves 4

Spinach Salad

2 bunches of fresh spinach

4 ounces Tofu Feta (see next page)

¼ cup olive oil

1 clove garlic, minced

½ small purple onion, quartered
   and thinly sliced

½ cup sun-dried tomatoes, soaked
   in hot water for about 10
   minutes, drained, and chopped
   (optional)

½ cup finely chopped fresh basil
   or mint

3 tablespoons balsamic vinegar

To prepare the salad, stem and clean the spinach, rinsing it twice. Spin the spinach dry in a salad spinner or blot with a paper towel. Place in the refrigerator.

Heat the ¼ cup of olive oil in a cast-iron skillet. When hot but not smoking, toss in the garlic and roast briefly. Place the spinach in a salad bowl. Pour the hot oil and garlic over it, tossing well to wilt the spinach. Add the Tofu Feta, onion, optional sun-dried tomatoes, basil, and vinegar. Toss lightly and serve.

Variation: Replace the Tofu Feta with 4 ounces crumbled feta cheese.

This is the most delicious and popular salad that we serve at Shoshoni. People enjoy it just as much whether using Tofu Feta or regular feta cheese.

Tofu Feta

½ pound firm tofu

1 tablespoon olive oil

1 tablespoon rice vinegar or fresh lemon juice

¼ teaspoon grated nutmeg

¼ teaspoon dried dill

Salt and pepper

To prepare the Tofu Feta, place the tofu in a small bowl and mash with a fork. Add the 1 tablespoon of olive oil, vinegar, nutmeg, dill, and salt and pepper to taste. Blend well. Cover and set aside.

Warm Beet and Carrot Salad with Fresh Mint

Serves 4 to 6

The rich flavors and colors of this dish are a warming addition to an autumn or winter meal.

4 large beets without tops

2 carrots, peeled and sliced diagonally

3 tablespoons minced fresh mint

3 tablespoons pure maple syrup

1 tablespoon ghee

Scrub the beets well and place them in a saucepan with just enough water to cover. Bring to a boil, cover, reduce the heat, and cook for 20 to 30 minutes or until the beets are fork tender.

Steam the carrots separately until tender. When the beets are done, peel and discard the outer skin (it should come off easily just using your fingers) and chop the beets coarsely. Combine the mint, maple syrup, and ghee in a small bowl and stir to mix well. Pour over the vegetables and toss gently. Serve warm.

Dressings, Chutneys, Sauces, Condiments

Salad Dressings

Chutneys

Sauces and Condiments

Balsamic Dijon Vinaigrette

Makes about 1¼ cups

Balsamic vinegar contributes to the earthy sweetness of this recipe. It is a staple salad dressing in our kitchen.

Combine all the ingredients in a pitcher. Whisk until well combined. Allow the dressing to sit for at least 1 hour before serving for the best flavor.

³/₄ cup olive oil

¼ cup water

2 tablespoons balsamic vinegar

2 tablespoons minced fresh parsley

1 tablespoon Dijon or stone-ground mustard

1 tablespoon minced fresh rosemary or dill, or 1 teaspoon dried rosemary or dill

2 teaspoons honey

1 garlic clove, minced

Salt and pepper

Creamy Pumpkin Seed Dressing

Pumpkin seeds are very high in protein and also have a delicious flavor. This dressing will give your salad an extra nutritional punch.

Combine the water, pumpkin seeds, oil, vinegar, salt, honey, and pepper in a blender and process until smooth and creamy. Stir in the chopped parsley and chill for at least 1 hour before serving.

3/4 cup water

1/2 cup raw pumpkin seeds

1/4 cup light sunflower oil

1/4 cup brown rice vinegar

1 teaspoon salt

1 teaspoon honey

1/2 teaspoon pepper

1/3 cup chopped fresh parsley

Dairy-Free Ranch Dressing

Ranch dressing is an all-time favorite. This version tastes so delicious you won't miss the buttermilk and mayonnaise. Silken tofu is high in protein and lends itself well to the flavors of the roasted garlic and spices.

Heat the oil in a skillet until very hot. Drop in the garlic and cook until browned. Transfer the oil and garlic to a blender along with the tofu, water, vinegar, honey, and pepper and process until smooth. Add the fresh or dried herbs, parsley, scallions, and salt to taste. Pulse the blender a few times, just until mixed. Pour into a pitcher and chill before serving.

1/2 cup olive oil

1 clove garlic, minced

1 package (about 12 ounces) firm silken tofu

1/4 to 1/2 cup water

1/4 cup apple cider vinegar

1 tablespoon honey

1/4 teaspoon pepper

1/4 cup fresh basil or a combination of fresh basil, oregano, dill, and sage, or 4 teaspoons dried herbs

2 tablespoons minced fresh parsley

2 tablespoons minced scallions

Salt

Fresh Mint and Carrot Dressing

Makes about 1 1/2 cups

This delicious dressing is similar to a French dressing but with a milder flavor.

Combine the carrots, oil, vinegar, lemon juice, honey, and garlic in a blender and process until smooth. Stir in the mint and salt and pepper to taste. Cover and chill before serving.

1 cup cooked carrots

1/4 cup sunflower oil

1/4 cup apple cider vinegar

2 tablespoons fresh lemon juice

1 tablespoon honey

1 clove garlic

1/3 cup chopped fresh mint

Salt and pepper

Moroccan Vinaigrette

This dressing has a lovely flavor for fresh garden salads or grain salads. Try it on rice, quinoa, or millet salads or just as a spicy alternative to your usual salad dressing.

Whisk the lime juice, paprika, mustard, coriander, ginger, honey, cumin, garlic, and salt and pepper to taste in a small bowl until well combined. Slowly whisk in the oil, beating constantly to make a smooth, thick dressing. Refrigerate until ready to use.

3 tablespoons fresh lime juice

2 teaspoons paprika

2 teaspoons ground coriander

2 teaspoons stone-ground mustard

2 teaspoons minced fresh ginger

2 teaspoons honey

1 teaspoon ground cumin

1 small clove garlic, minced

Salt and pepper

3/4 cup sunflower oil or olive oil

Yogurt Parmesan Dressing

Our guests love this tart and creamy dressing.

Combine the yogurt, optional egg, cheese, vinegar, herbs, honey, garlic, salt, and pepper in a blender and process briefly. While blending, add the oil in a slow, steady stream to gradually thicken the dressing. Will keep at least two weeks in the refrigerator.

1 cup plain yogurt

1 egg (optional)

3 tablespoons freshly grated
  Parmesan cheese

2 tablespoons apple cider vinegar

1 tablespoon fresh basil,
  or 1 teaspoon dried basil

1 tablespoon fresh oregano,
  or 1 teaspoon dried oregano

1 tablespoon honey

1 clove garlic, minced

1/4 teaspoon salt

Pinch of pepper

1/2 cup olive oil

Zesty Lemon and Yogurt Dressing

Makes about 1¹/₂ cups

We are a creative bunch in the Shoshoni kitchen. Every day another idea is born. The lemon zest in this recipe makes a refreshing, light dressing.

Combine the oil, lemon juice, dill, lemon zest, honey, and pepper in a blender. Process until well combined. Add the yogurt and salt to taste. Pulse briefly, just until mixed. Serve chilled.

¹/₂ cup sunflower oil

3 tablespoons fresh lemon juice

2 tablespoons fresh dill,
  or ¹/₂ teaspoon dried dill

1 tablespoon lemon zest

1 tablespoon honey

¹/₂ teaspoon pepper

1 cup plain yogurt

Salt to taste

Fresh Basil and Apricot Chutney

Makes 2³/4 cups

We use fresh basil from our Eldorado Ashram garden for this tasty fruit chutney. Use the same amount of fresh cilantro for an equally delicious variation.

Place all of the ingredients in a food processor fitted with a metal blade and blend into a smooth paste.

2 cups packed fresh basil

¹/2 cup flaked coconut

¹/4 cup dried apricots, soaked in
  hot water until soft and drained

3 tablespoons sesame seeds

1 tablespoon granulated fructose or
  honey

2 teaspoons minced fresh ginger

1 tablespoon fresh lemon juice

1 tablespoon orange juice

Pinch of salt

Fresh Coconut and Green Chili Chutney

Makes 1¹/₂ to 2 cups

This chutney is also a great dipping sauce for Vegetable Pakoras, page 164. For a thinner sauce, add a little yogurt.

Place all the ingredients in a blender or food processor and grind until smooth. Chill until ready to use.

1 cup grated fresh coconut and the coconut milk, or 1 cup unsweetened, dried coconut and 1 cup of canned coconut milk

^{1}/$_3$ cup fresh mint

^{1}/$_3$ cup chopped fresh cilantro

10 blanched whole almonds

2 tablespoons fresh lime juice

1 tablespoon grated fresh ginger

1 tablespoon Sucanat or pure maple syrup (optional)

1 or 2 jalapeno chilies, seeded and chopped

Fresh Ginger and Date Chutney

No Indian meal is complete without the addition of chutney. This fresh chutney requires no cooking. It can be prepared quickly and easily with delicious results.

Place all the ingredients in a food processor fitted with a metal blade and process into a fine paste. Serve cold on the side with your favorite curry.

1/2 cup minced fresh ginger

1/2 cup flaked coconut

1/2 cup fresh cilantro or mint

1/4 cup pitted dates

1 tablespoon fresh lemon juice

1 tablespoon orange juice

1 tablespoon honey

Pinch of salt

Pinch of cayenne

Holiday Cranberry Walnut Chutney

With this festive chutney you can take advantage of the fresh cranberries that are sold in the market during the fall holiday season. It goes very well with Indian food, but don't feel limited. It makes a nice presentation and the flavors will enhance any kind of holiday meal.

Heat the ghee in a saucepan. Add the ginger and sauté it briefly. Stir in the fresh cranberries, orange juice, dried cranberries, sweetener, orange zest, cinnamon stick, nutmeg, and clove. Reduce the heat to low and simmer for 30 minutes, stirring frequently to prevent the mixture from scorching. When the cranberries have cooked down and softened, stir in the walnuts. Remove the cinnamon stick and clove. Serve warm or chilled.

1 tablespoon ghee

1 tablespoon minced fresh ginger

2 cups fresh cranberries

2 cups fresh orange juice

1 cup unsweetened dried cranberries

1 cup natural sweetener (such as Sucanat, granulated fructose, or raw sugar)

2 tablespoons grated orange zest

1 cinnamon stick

1/2 teaspoon grated nutmeg

1 whole clove

1/2 cup chopped walnuts

Spicy Plum Chutney

Ripe plums make a delicious variation of chutney.

3 tablespoons ghee

1/2 teaspoon whole fennel seeds

2 tablespoons orange zest

1 1/2 teaspoons minced fresh ginger

1 1/2 pounds firm ripe plums,
  halved, pitted, and quartered

1 1/2 cups natural sugar

1/4 teaspoon ground cloves

1/4 teaspoon ground cinnamon

1/4 teaspoon ground coriander

1/2 cup dried ribbon coconut

Pinch of salt

Heat the ghee in a heavy saucepan over low heat. Stir in the fennel seeds and brown them lightly. Add the orange zest and ginger and cook for 1 to 2 minutes. Stir in the plums, sugar, cloves, cinnamon, and coriander. Raise the heat and bring to a boil, stirring constantly. Reduce the heat to low and cook until the chutney is thick and glazed, about 30 minutes. Stir in the coconut and salt. Chill before serving.

Sweet Fennel and Tomato Chutney

Makes about 3 cups

This cooked chutney is sweet and delicious. Fennel seeds help cool the hot nature of the tomatoes to make a delicious condiment for an Indian feast.

1 tablespoon ghee

2 teaspoons whole cumin seeds

1 teaspoon whole fennel seeds

4 cups chopped fresh tomatoes

1/2 cup Sucanat or other natural sugar

1 teaspoon ground coriander

1 teaspoon Garam Masala, page 70

1/4 cup chopped fresh cilantro

1/2 teaspoon salt

Heat the ghee in a saucepan. Add the cumin and fennel seeds and cook until lightly browned and fragrant. Add the tomatoes, sugar, coriander, and Garam Masala. Stir well and simmer on low for 15 minutes. Stir in the cilantro and salt. Serve warm or chilled.

Curry Cottage Cheese Sauce

Makes about 1 cup

This mild curry sauce goes especially well over Asparagus Koftas, page 18, but it also can be used to turn simple steamed green beans, cauliflower, or asparagus into an elegant and tasty side dish.

Heat the ghee in a skillet. Add the scallion and briefly sauté. Stir in the curry powder and sauté for 1 minute. Remove from the heat.

1 tablespoon ghee

¼ cup minced scallions

1 teaspoon curry powder

1 cup low-fat cottage cheese

1 tablespoon natural sugar

1 teaspoon salt

1 teaspoon fresh lemon juice

¼ teaspoon grated nutmeg

Combine the cottage cheese, sugar, salt, lemon juice, and nutmeg in a blender and process until smooth. Using a rubber spatula, add the scallions and oil from the skillet. Pulse the blender once or twice to mix. Pour the sauce into a small saucepan and warm on very low heat. Do not boil as the sauce will curdle. Immediately remove from the heat once the sauce is warm.

Coriander Spiced Yogurt

Makes 2 cups

We have used this simple spiced yogurt with Millet Croquettes, page 24, and Sesame Spinach Dal Badis, page 27. It also is very good on the side of any Indian curry dish.

2 cups plain yogurt

2 teaspoons ground coriander

1 teaspoon dried dill

$\frac{1}{2}$ teaspoon turmeric

$\frac{1}{4}$ teaspoon salt

Combine all the ingredients in a bowl and gently stir until well blended. Serve chilled.

Cucumber Mint Raita

Makes 2 to 3 cups

Raita is another indispensable accompaniment to an Indian feast. It is delicious with our Homemade Urad Dal Patties, page 22, or Sesame Spinach Dal Badis, page 27.

2 cups plain yogurt

$\frac{1}{2}$ cup peeled, seeded, and grated cucumber

$\frac{1}{4}$ cup grated carrot

3 tablespoons minced fresh mint

1 teaspoon ground coriander

Combine all the ingredients in a bowl and gently stir until well mixed. Serve chilled.

Fresh Hoisin Sauce

Makes 2$\frac{1}{2}$ cups, enough for 10 servings of Moo Shoo

This sauce is a new twist on the traditional. It's delicious with our Crisp Moo Shoo with Homemade Scallion Pancakes, page 104.

Combine all the ingredients in a saucepan and bring to a boil. Lower the heat, cover, and cook over low to medium heat for 20 to 25 minutes. Remove from the heat and transfer to a blender. Process into a smooth sauce. If you prefer a thinner sauce, dilute with a little more apple juice.

1 cup pitted prunes or dried apricots

$\frac{1}{2}$ cup natural soy sauce or Bragg Liquid Aminos

$\frac{1}{2}$ cup apple juice

$\frac{1}{4}$ cup rice vinegar

$\frac{1}{4}$ cup Sucanat, granulated fructose, or honey

1 tablespoon minced fresh ginger

$\frac{1}{2}$ hot chili, seeded and minced (optional)

Ghee

This recipe starts with two pounds of butter; however, you can use any amount of butter depending on how much ghee you would like to make. For example, we start with sixteen pounds of butter, which makes about one and one-half gallons of ghee. The more butter you start with, the bigger the pot you will need.

2 pounds unsalted butter, preferably organic

Strainer

Cheesecloth or a thin, flat cloth

Extra pot

1 pint-size, clear glass jar with a tight-fitting lid

Place the butter in a heavy-bottomed, 4-quart saucepan. A cast-iron kettle is great if you have one. Melt the butter over moderate heat. When the butter has melted, increase the heat and bring to a boil. Reduce the heat to very low.

Allow the butter to simmer slowly, uncovered and undisturbed until the milk solids have settled on the bottom of the pot and turned from white to golden brown. A thin crust will be floating on top of the transparent butterfat. The butterfat should be a rich golden brown. If the temperature gets too high or the butter cooks too long the butterfat will turn a dark, toasted brown color.

Remove the ghee from the stove away from the heat. Line the strainer with several layers of cheesecloth. Place the strainer over the extra pot. Ladle the ghee into the strainer trying not to disturb the milk solids on the bottom.

Allow the ghee to cool uncovered until it reaches room temperature. Pour into the glass jar and close with a tight-fitting lid. Store the ghee in a cool place for up to two months. If you do not plan to use it immediately, store it in the refrigerator for up to four months.

Homemade Soy Mayonnaise

The joy of creating with soy! This recipe is especially satisfying for dairy-sensitive people and can be used wherever you would use real mayonnaise. It is the secret to our tasty potato salads and Tempeh Salad, page 35. We also use it as a side condiment with veggie burgers.

Combine the tofu, oil, lemon juice, salt, garlic, pepper, and nutmeg in a food processor and blend until smooth and creamy. Add the scallions and pulse once or twice to mix.

1 package (about 12 ounces)
  extra-firm silken tofu

1/3 cup olive oil

3 tablespoons fresh lemon juice

1 teaspoon salt

1 clove garlic, or 1/2 teaspoon
  garlic powder

Pinch of pepper

Pinch of nutmeg

1/4 cup chopped scallions
  or fresh chives

Zesty Mango Salsa

Makes 3 cups

*This recipe is easy to vary using other fruits such as pineapple or papaya.
Have fun and try them all!*

2 cups diced firm red tomatoes

1 ripe mango, peeled and diced
(1 cup)

1/2 small purple onion,
finely chopped

1/4 to 1/2 cup minced fresh
cilantro

3 tablespoons fresh lime juice

1/2 teaspoon salt

1 teaspoon minced habanero or
serrano pepper (optional)

Combine all the ingredients in a bowl and let stand 30 minutes. Adjust seasonings to taste.

Marinated Ginger

Makes 1 cup

*Marinated fresh ginger is a traditional accompaniment to sushi. Try this
recipe with our Shoshoni-Style Nori Rolls, page 136.*

1 cup peeled and thinly sliced
fresh ginger

1 cup water

1/2 cup granulated fructose
or honey

1/4 cup raspberry or plum vinegar

Pinch of salt

Combine all the ingredients in a saucepan. Cover and bring to a boil. Lower the heat and cook uncovered for 15 minutes or until the liquid has reduced to half. Transfer to a bowl and chill in the refrigerator.

Roasted Peanut Dipping Sauce

This recipe is delicious with any stir-fry, but it is an especially tasty dipping sauce with Thai Spring Rolls with Spicy Fresh Basil, page 28.

Combine the water, Sucanat, peanut butter, vinegar, Bragg Liquid Aminos, cornstarch, and chili in a small saucepan. Bring to a boil and cook, stirring constantly, until thickened. Stir in the peanuts and serve.

1/2 cup water

1/4 cup Sucanat or other natural sugar

3 tablespoons natural peanut butter

2 tablespoons rice vinegar

1 tablespoon Bragg Liquid Aminos or natural soy sauce

1 tablespoon cornstarch

2 teaspoons minced fresh red or green chili

1/4 cup roasted peanuts, coarsely chopped

Tofu Ricotta

This is a great alternative to cottage, ricotta, or feta cheese for those who wish to avoid dairy products or want to experiment with a new taste.

Combine half the tofu and all the remaining ingredients in a food processor, and process until smooth. In a small bowl, mash the remaining tofu with a fork and stir into the blended mixture.

1 pound firm tofu

1 tablespoon fresh lemon juice

1 teaspoon salt

1 teaspoon garlic powder

Tofu Feta Variation

Makes about 2 cups

This is a delicious dairy-free alternative to feta cheese. For a version that uses less oil, see page 43.

*C*ombine half the tofu and all of the remaining ingredients in a food processor. Process until smooth. In a small bowl, mash the remaining tofu with a fork and stir into the blended mixture. Adjust seasonings to taste and refrigerate.

1 pound firm tofu

2 tablespoons fresh lemon juice

1 tablespoon minced chives

1 teaspoon salt

1 teaspoon garlic powder

1 tablespoon minced fresh dill, or
   1 teaspoon dried dill

1 teaspoon olive oil

Roasted Red Pepper Sauce

Makes 2 cups

This incredibly versatile sauce is used in many of our Italian recipes that would normally call for tomato sauce. If you plan to use this sauce by itself over pasta, consider adding some sautéed onion, garlic, and herbs of your choice, such as fresh or dried basil, oregano, thyme, or rosemary.

3 whole red bell peppers

1 cup water

Salt and pepper

Place the whole peppers directly over a gas burner. If you don't have a gas stove, place the peppers on a baking sheet in a preheated 450°F oven and bake for about 45 minutes or until the outer skin is blackened. Turn the peppers occasionally to cook them evenly. When the entire pepper is charred, remove from the flame (or the oven) and set aside to cool.

Rub the charred skin off the peppers. Avoid using water so that the roasted flavor isn't washed away. You don't have to remove every bit of the charred skin. Cut open the peppers and remove the stem and seeds. Place the peppers in a blender with a small amount of the water—use just enough to make a smooth, velvety sauce. Season with salt and pepper to taste.

Note: If you prefer not to roast your own peppers, 1 (8-ounce) jar of roasted red peppers (enough to equal 1 cup) may be substituted for the fresh red bell peppers. Just remove any seeds and ribs and blend with the water as directed.

Masalas

A masala is a mixture of spices used to create a certain flavor or character in your dish. Don't feel limited in expressing your creativity with masala blends. There are many well-established masalas in Indian cooking and there are some great masalas that are beneficial for therapeutic use in your Ayurvedic cooking. Dosha-specific mixtures often are called churnas. You can add them last in your dish or use them as a condiment on any or all of the dishes in your meal. Masalas should be stored at room temperature in an airtight container, just as you would keep any other spices.

Garam Masala

There are many combinations of this classic masala. It is a warming and sweet mix of spices that originated in the north of India. Vata and Kapha can use this mixture, but Pitta should avoid it, especially in the summer months, as the ginger and black pepper can be overly heating for the Pitta constitution.

Roast the cumin and coriander seeds in a dry skillet until they emit a nutty aroma. Transfer to a spice grinder along with the cinnamon, bay leaves, cardamom seeds, ginger, cloves, peppercorns, and nutmeg and process into a fine powder.

2 tablespoons whole cumin seeds

2 tablespoons whole coriander seeds

2 teaspoons ground cinnamon

2 bay leaves

1 teaspoon whole cardamom seeds

1 teaspoon ground ginger

½ teaspoon ground cloves

½ teaspoon black peppercorns

½ teaspoon grated nutmeg

Kapha Spice

Makes about 1/2 cup

The ginger, hot pepper, and cloves in this blend help stimulate the sluggish Kapha constitution.

Roast the cumin, coriander, and fenugreek seeds in a dry skillet until they emit a nutty aroma. Transfer to a spice grinder along with the remaining ingredients and process into a fine powder.

2 tablespoons whole cumin seeds

2 tablespoons whole coriander seeds

2 teaspoons whole fenugreek seeds

1 teaspoon ground ginger

1 teaspoon turmeric

1/4 teaspoon hot red pepper flakes (optional for spicier mix)

1/4 teaspoon ground cloves

Pitta Spice

A cooling blend of spices to settle overheated Pitta.

2 tablespoons whole cumin seeds

2 tablespoons whole coriander
   seeds

2 tablespoons whole fennel seeds

2 tablespoons turmeric

Combine all the ingredients in a spice grinder and process into a fine powder.

Rasam Masala

Makes ½ cup

A spicy blend to fire up a sluggish Kapha digestion. Vatas should use it sparingly and Pittas should avoid it completely. The red and black pepper can be overly stimulating for these doshas.

2 tablespoons whole black
   mustard seeds

2 tablespoons whole cumin seeds

2 tablespoons whole coriander
   seeds

2 tablespoons whole black
   peppercorns

2 tablespoons hot red pepper
   flakes

Roast the mustard, cumin, and coriander seeds in a dry skillet until they emit a nutty aroma. Transfer to a spice grinder along with the peppercorns and red pepper flakes and process into a fine powder.

Vata Spice

This spice blend with ground licorice, coriander, and cardamom has a calming effect on a sensitive nervous system.

2 tablespoons whole cumin seeds

2 tablespoons whole coriander seeds

½ teaspoon whole cardamom seeds

1 teaspoon ground licorice

½ teaspoon ground ginger

¼ teaspoon asafetida

¼ teaspoon salt

Roast the cumin and coriander seeds in a dry skillet until they emit a nutty aroma. Transfer to a spice grinder along with the cardamom seeds and process into a powder. Stir in the ground licorice, ginger, asafetida, and salt.

Madras-Style Curry Powder

This is a flavorful, basic curry powder that can be added to many vegetable dishes to perk up the flavor.

Combine all of the ingredients in a small bowl and stir until well blended. Store in a glass jar with a tight-fitting lid.

¹/₄ cup ground cumin

¹/₄ cup ground coriander

¹/₄ cup turmeric

6 to 8 broken bay leaves

1 teaspoon cayenne

1 teaspoon ground fennel

Yoga Kitchen

Soups and Stews

Dal Soups

Vegetable and Bean Soups

Adzuki Bean Dal with Fresh Garden Greens

Adzuki beans have a deep, sweet, earthy flavor. In Ayurvedic cooking they are considered nourishing and cleansing for the body.

Heat the ghee in a large saucepan. Add the cumin seeds, asafetida, and turmeric and sauté for just a second. Add the onion, ginger, and green chili and sauté for 5 minutes. Add the 4 cups of water or vegetable stock, the cooked or canned beans, carrots, and bay leaves. Bring to a boil. Reduce the heat, cover, and cook for 30 minutes for the flavors to blend.

Stir in the greens, coriander, and salt. Let the dal rest covered for 10 minutes before serving so the greens can wilt. Remove the bay leaves before serving.

Note: To prepare dried beans, soak 1 cup dried adzuki beans in 3 to 4 cups water overnight. When you are ready to cook the beans, drain off the soaking water and rinse with fresh water. Place the beans in a heavy-bottomed soup pot with 6 cups of fresh water or vegetable stock. Bring to a boil, cover, lower the heat, and simmer for about 2 hours or until the beans are tender.

Adzuki beans are very high in fiber and can take a while to cook. Alternatively, you may cook the soaked beans in a pressure cooker with 6 cups of water for 1 hour at low pressure (after they have reached full pressure). Canned organic beans are a fine substitute if you are short on time.

1 tablespoon ghee

1 teaspoon whole cumin seeds

1/2 teaspoon asafetida

1/2 teaspoon turmeric

1/2 small onion, minced

1 tablespoon minced fresh ginger

1/2 fresh green chili, seeded and minced

4 cups water or vegetable stock

2 cups cooked adzuki beans, or 1 (15-ounce) can organic adzuki beans (see note)

1 cup chopped carrots

2 bay leaves

2 cups stemmed and chopped fresh greens (such as kale, collards, or spinach)

1 teaspoon ground coriander

1 teaspoon salt

Chowla Dal (Black-Eyed Peas) with Louki Squash

Serves 4 to 6

Chowla dal is more commonly known as the black-eyed pea.

Heat the ghee in a large saucepan. Add the cumin seeds, asafetida, and turmeric and brown them for a second. Add the onion and sauté for 5 minutes. Add the black-eyed peas and their cooking liquid (if using canned beans, add 4 cups of water or vegetable stock) and squash and bring to a boil. Reduce the heat, cover, and simmer for 20 minutes or until the vegetables are tender and the flavors have blended. Stir in the cilantro, coriander, Rasam Masala, and salt.

Note: To prepare dried beans, soak 1 cup dried black-eyed peas in 3 to 4 cups water overnight. When you are ready to cook the beans, drain off the soaking water and rinse with fresh water. Place the beans in a heavy-bottomed soup pot with 6 cups of fresh water or vegetable stock. Bring to a boil, cover, lower the heat, and simmer for about 1 hour or until the beans are tender. Canned organic beans are a fine substitute if you are short on time.

1 tablespoon ghee

2 teaspoons whole cumin seeds

1/2 teaspoon asafetida

1/2 teaspoon turmeric

1 onion, finely chopped

4 cups water or vegetable stock (add only if using canned beans)

2 cups cooked black-eyed peas, or 1 (15-ounce) can organic black-eyed peas (see note)

1 cup diced louki squash (available at Asian markets) or zucchini

1/4 cup chopped fresh cilantro

1 teaspoon ground coriander

1/2 teaspoon Rasam Masala, page 72

1/2 teaspoon salt

Curried Chickpea and Potato Stew

Serves 6

This hearty stew is simple and mildly spiced.

Rinse and drain the soaked beans. Place them in a large saucepan with the water or vegetable stock, bay leaves, and asafetida. Bring to a boil, reduce the heat, cover, and simmer for 2 hours or until the beans are tender. If using canned chickpeas, simmer for 10 minutes to allow the flavors to blend.

Heat the ghee in a skillet. Add the cumin and turmeric and brown for 1 minute. Add the potatoes and sauté for 5 minutes. When the beans are done, stir in the potatoes, cover, and simmer until the potatoes are soft and the stew is thick, about 30 minutes. Stir in the salt, coriander, and cumin and mix well. Garnish with the fresh cilantro.

1 cup dried chickpeas soaked in water overnight, or 1 (15-ounce) can chickpeas

4 cups water or vegetable stock

2 bay leaves

$1/4$ teaspoon asafetida

2 teaspoons ghee

1 teaspoon whole cumin seeds

$1/2$ teaspoon turmeric

3 cups peeled and chopped potatoes

1 teaspoon salt

1 teaspoon ground coriander

$1/2$ teaspoon ground cumin

$1/4$ cup chopped fresh cilantro

Golden Mung Dal Sambar with Coconut Milk

Serves 6

This bright, sunny soup adds flair to any Indian meal.

Sort through the dal to remove any stones or foreign material. Rinse and drain.

1 cup golden mung dal

1 tablespoon ghee

2 teaspoons whole cumin seeds

1/2 teaspoon turmeric

Pinch of asafetida

4 cups water

1 cup chopped carrots

1/2 cup sliced fresh green beans
  (cut in 1-inch lengths)

1 bay leaf

1 cup fresh, frozen, or canned
  coconut milk

1/4 cup chopped fresh cilantro

2 teaspoons salt

1 teaspoon sambar spice (available
  at Indian markets)

Heat the ghee in a large saucepan. Add the cumin seeds, turmeric, and asafetida and sauté for 1 minute. Add the dal, water, carrots, green beans, and bay leaf. Bring to a boil, reduce the heat, cover, and cook for 30 minutes or until the dal is tender. Stir in the coconut milk, cilantro, salt, and sambar spice and serve.

Toor Dal with Potatoes and Eggplant

This is one of Swamiji's favorites.

Rinse and drain the dal. Heat the ghee in a saucepan until very hot. Add the mustard and cumin seeds and cover. When the seeds begin to pop, immediately lower the heat and stir in the onion, ginger, chili, asafetida, and turmeric. Sauté for 1 minute. Add the rinsed dal, water, potatoes, eggplant, and bay leaves. Bring to a boil, reduce the heat, cover, and simmer for 30 to 40 minutes. When the beans are tender, stir in the cilantro and season with salt to taste.

1 cup toor dal

1 tablespoon ghee

2 teaspoons whole black mustard seeds

2 teaspoons whole cumin seeds

1/2 onion, finely chopped

2 tablespoons minced fresh ginger

1/2 hot green chili, seeded and minced

1/2 teaspoon asafetida

1/2 teaspoon turmeric

4 cups water

4 cups peeled and chopped potatoes

1 cup chopped Japanese eggplant

2 bay leaves

1/4 cup chopped fresh cilantro

1 to 2 teaspoons salt

Warming Whole Mung Dal with Winter Squash

Whole mung beans have a deep, satisfying flavor.

1 tablespoon ghee

2 teaspoons whole black mustard seeds

1 onion, finely chopped

½ teaspoon turmeric

½ teaspoon asafetida

2 cups cooked mung beans (1 cup dried), or 1 (15-ounce) can organic mung beans (see note)

4 cups water or vegetable stock (add only if using canned beans)

1 cup peeled and chopped pumpkin or other winter squash

1 tablespoon fresh lime juice

2 teaspoons curry powder

1 to 2 teaspoons salt

1 teaspoon ground coriander

Heat the ghee in a large saucepan until very hot. Add the mustard seeds, cover, and wait for the seeds to begin popping. Immediately lower the heat and add the onion, turmeric, and asafetida. Sauté for 1 minute. Add the beans and their cooking liquid (if using canned beans, add them along with 4 cups water or vegetable stock) and the squash. Bring to a boil, reduce the heat, cover, and simmer for 20 minutes or until the squash is tender and the flavors have blended. Stir in the lime juice, curry powder, salt to taste, and coriander.

Note: To prepare dried beans, soak 1 cup dried mung beans in 3 to 4 cups water overnight. When you are ready to cook the beans, drain off the soaking water and rinse with fresh water. Place the beans in a heavy-bottomed soup pot with 6 cups of fresh water or vegetable stock. Bring to a boil, cover, lower the heat, and simmer for about 1 hour or until the beans are tender. Canned mung beans may be substituted if you are short on time.

Adzuki Bean and Roasted Red Pepper Minestrone

Serves 6 to 8

2 cups cooked adzuki beans (1 cup dried), or 1 (15-ounce) can organic adzuki beans

5 cups water or vegetable stock

4 whole sprigs of parsley

2 bay leaves

2 large sprigs of rosemary

2 tablespoons ghee

1 onion, finely chopped

2 cloves garlic, minced

1 cup diced carrots

1 cup peeled and diced winter squash (such as butternut, pumpkin, or acorn)

1/2 cup chopped green beans

1/2 green bell pepper, diced

1/2 cup chopped fresh basil, or 2 teaspoons dried basil

1 teaspoon dried oregano

1 teaspoon dried thyme

2 cups Roasted Red Pepper Sauce, page 68

3 tablespoons chopped fresh parsley

2 teaspoons salt

1/2 teaspoon pepper

1 cup cooked rainbow-colored pasta shells

Minestrone lends itself to many interpretations. This recipe uses Roasted Red Pepper Sauce, page 68, for a tasty soup base.

To prepare dried beans, soak 1 cup dried adzuki beans in 3 to 4 cups water overnight. When you are ready to cook the beans, drain off the soaking water and rinse with fresh water. Place the beans in a heavy-bottomed soup pot with 5 cups of fresh water or vegetable stock. Add the whole sprigs of parsley, bay leaves, and rosemary. Bring to a boil, cover, lower the heat, and simmer for about 1 hour or until the beans are tender. Alternatively, the beans may be pressure cooked for 1 hour at low pressure (after high pressure has been reached). Canned organic beans may be substituted if you are short on time.

Heat the ghee in a separate pot. Add the onion and garlic and sauté for 5 minutes. Add the carrots, squash, green beans, green pepper, basil, oregano, and thyme. Sauté 5 more minutes, then stir the vegetables into the pot with the cooked adzuki beans. (If you are using canned beans, add the 5 cups water or stock now.) Cover and simmer for 15 minutes or until the vegetables are tender.

Stir the Roasted Red Pepper Sauce into the soup along with the chopped parsley, salt, and pepper. Add the pasta to each bowl of soup just before serving.

Autumn Vegetable Chowder

You will never miss the cream in this dairy-free vegetable chowder. The creamy cauliflower and potato base, mixed with a bounty of fresh garden vegetables, makes a hearty main dish soup.

2 tablespoons ghee or sunflower oil

1 small onion, finely chopped

4 cups vegetable stock or water

2 cups cauliflower florets

2 cups peeled and chopped potatoes (cut in medium chunks)

1 cup trimmed and cut green beans (in 1-inch lengths)

1/2 cup chopped carrots

2 teaspoons whole cumin seeds

1/2 cup thinly sliced red bell pepper

1 tablespoon fresh lemon juice

1 teaspoon ground coriander

Salt and pepper

3 tablespoons minced fresh parsley

Heat 1 tablespoon of the ghee in a soup pot. Add the onion and sauté until translucent. Add the vegetable stock, cauliflower, and potatoes. Bring to a boil, reduce the heat, cover, and simmer about 10 minutes or until tender.

Meanwhile, steam the green beans and carrots until tender. When the cauliflower and potatoes are tender, blend half of them with some of the cooking water until smooth and creamy and stir back into the soup pot. Then stir in the steamed green beans and carrots.

Heat the remaining 1 tablespoon of ghee in a skillet. Add the cumin seeds and sauté until lightly browned. Add the red bell pepper and sauté 2 to 3 minutes or until just tender. Stir into the soup. Season with the lemon juice, coriander, and salt and pepper to taste. Garnish with the fresh parsley just before serving.

Cajun-Style Louisiana Gumbo

Shanti created this dish while reminiscing about the delicious Cajun food her grandmother cooked. Traditionally made with a browned roux and combinations of seafood, chicken, and sausage, gumbo is a staple in southwest Louisiana. This version uses a dry-roasted roux instead of an oil-based one, flavorful vegetables, and vegetarian sausage for authentic flavor.

Dry-roast the flour in a cast-iron skillet over medium heat, whisking frequently until it is a dark beige color. While the flour is browning, heat the ghee in a saucepan. Add the onion and garlic and sauté for 5 minutes. Stir in the optional vegetarian sausage, scallions, celery, and chili. Sauté until the sausage is browned. Add the okra, bell pepper, corn, carrots, paprika, and browned flour. Stir to coat the vegetables with the flour. Add the water and bring to a boil. Reduce the heat, cover, and simmer on low to medium heat for 45 minutes. Stir in the parsley, Bragg Liquid Aminos, vegetable broth powder, salt to taste, and cayenne.

5 tablespoons unbleached white flour

2 tablespoons ghee

1 onion, finely chopped

1 clove garlic, minced

1/2 cup vegetarian sausage (optional)

1/2 cup chopped scallions

1 stalk celery, chopped

1/2 green chili, seeded and minced

1 cup chopped fresh or frozen okra

1 red bell pepper, chopped

1/2 cup fresh or frozen corn kernels

1/2 cup chopped carrots

1 tablespoon paprika

6 cups water

1/2 cup chopped fresh parsley

1/4 cup Bragg Liquid Aminos or
   natural soy sauce

1 tablespoon vegetable broth powder

1 to 2 teaspoons salt

1/4 teaspoon cayenne

Chilled Lime and Honeydew Soup

Faith's favorite refreshing and cooling summertime soup.

Purée the melon in a blender along with the apple and lime juice. Transfer the mixture to a serving bowl and stir in the sour cream and ginger. Serve well chilled. Garnish individual servings with a thin slice of lime and a sprig of fresh mint, if desired.

1 honeydew melon, peeled, seeded, and chopped

1 cup apple juice

$1/3$ cup fresh lime juice

$1/2$ cup sour cream

1 teaspoon grated fresh ginger

Thin lime slices or mint sprigs, for garnish (optional)

Cream of Asparagus Soup

This soup is an elegant way to start off a holiday meal, or serve it as a meal in itself.

2 pounds fresh asparagus

5 cups vegetable stock or water

1 cup chopped leeks, white part only

1 stalk celery, thinly sliced

2 cups milk or plain soymilk

1/2 cup butter

1/2 cup unbleached white flour (or use spelt flour for wheat allergies)

1 tablespoon minced fresh tarragon, or 1 teaspoon dried tarragon

2 teaspoons salt

1/2 teaspoon pepper

Dash of Tabasco or a pinch of cayenne

Snap off and discard the tough ends of the asparagus and peel the stalks unless they are very tender. Chop the tender tips off the asparagus and set aside. Slice the stems into 1/2-inch pieces. Combine the asparagus stems, vegetable stock, leeks, and celery in a heavy-bottomed soup pot or saucepan. Bring to a simmer and cook until the vegetables are tender but not overcooked, about 20 to 30 minutes.

Purée the soup in a blender or food processor, return it to the pot, and stir in the reserved asparagus tips and the milk. Heat until steaming but do not boil.

While the vegetables are cooking, make a roux in a separate pan by melting the butter and gradually whisking in the flour. Cook over very low heat, stirring almost constantly for about 5 minutes or until the flour no longer tastes raw. Do not allow the flour to brown. Rapidly whisk the roux into the steaming soup. Stir until thickened and smooth. Season with the tarragon, salt, pepper, and Tabasco to taste. Let the soup stand at least 10 minutes before serving to allow the flavors to blend.

Cream of Broccoli and Cashew Soup

Serves 6

This wonderful recipe uses a creamy cashew base complemented by fresh garden dill to make a luxurious and nutritious soup.

2 tablespoons ghee

1 small onion, finely chopped

1 clove garlic, minced

4 cups fresh broccoli florets and peeled, finely chopped stems

5 cups vegetable stock or water

2 cups raw cashews

2 teaspoons dried dill

Salt and pepper

Heat the ghee in a heavy-bottomed soup pot. Add the onion and garlic and sauté until soft. Stir in the vegetable stock and broccoli. Cover and simmer for 10 minutes or until the broccoli is bright green and tender.

Reserve 2 cups of the cooked broccoli. Blend the remainder of the cooked broccoli with a little of the cooking stock until it is smooth. Stir the purée back into the soup pot.

Place the cashews in a blender with just enough soup to blend into a smooth sauce. Stir the blended cashews into the soup pot. Season with the dill and salt and pepper to taste. Stir in the reserved broccoli and serve.

Golden Pumpkin and Coconut Stew

The sweet, earthy flavor of pumpkin complemented with coconut is a perfect remedy for the cold-weather blues.

Heat the ghee in a saucepan. Add the onion, chili, and ginger and sauté for 5 minutes. Remove from the heat, stir in the turmeric, and set aside.

1 tablespoon ghee

1 onion, diced

1 tablespoon minced hot green chili

1 1/2 teaspoons minced fresh ginger

1 teaspoon turmeric

6 cups vegetable stock or water

1 stalk fresh lemongrass, chopped in 1-inch pieces, or 3 tablespoons dried lemongrass

2 1/2 pounds pumpkin, peeled and chopped

1 cup coconut milk

1/2 cup fresh or frozen green peas

1/4 cup chopped fresh cilantro

1 tablespoon natural sugar (optional)

2 teaspoons salt

Bring the stock to a boil in a large soup pot. Remove from the heat, add the lemongrass, and steep for 10 minutes. Add the pumpkin, bring to a boil, reduce the heat, cover, and cook for 10 minutes or until the pumpkin is tender. Purée half the mixture in a blender and return it to the soup pot. Stir in the coconut milk, peas, cilantro, optional sugar, and salt. Add the reserved onion, chili, ginger, and turmeric mixture, and stir to mix well. Heat gently and serve.

Herbed Vegetable Barley Soup

Barley is a light, sweet grain that makes a simple hearty soup.

Heat the ghee in a large soup pot. Add the onion and garlic and sauté until browned. Add the vegetable stock, squash, barley, carrots, bell pepper, celery, dill, rosemary, savory, and bay leaves. Bring to a boil, reduce the heat to medium-low, cover, and simmer for 30 to 40 minutes or until the barley is tender.

Stir in the spinach, parsley, optional broth powder, salt to taste, and pepper. Simmer 5 minutes longer or until the spinach is tender.

2 tablespoons ghee

1 medium onion, finely chopped

1 clove garlic, minced

5 cups vegetable stock or water

2 cups peeled and diced butternut squash

1 cup pearl barley, rinsed and drained

1 cup diced carrots

1/2 cup chopped red bell pepper

1 stalk celery, chopped

2 tablespoons minced fresh dill,
  or 2 teaspoons dried dill

1 tablespoon minced fresh rosemary,
  or 1 teaspoon dried rosemary

1 tablespoon fresh summer savory,
  or 1 teaspoon dried savory

2 bay leaves

1 cup fresh spinach or other greens,
  washed, stemmed, and chopped

1/4 cup chopped fresh parsley

1 tablespoon vegetable broth powder
  (optional, for added flavor)

1 to 2 teaspoons salt

1/2 teaspoon pepper

Mediterranean Red Lentil and Spinach Stew

This warming autumn or winter stew is delicious as an accompaniment to whole wheat couscous, cooked millet, or basmati rice for a simple dinner.

Heat the ghee in a saucepan. Add the onion and sauté until well browned and caramelized, about 10 minutes. Add the ginger and garlic and sauté for 2 minutes. Stir in the cumin, paprika, coriander, and cinnamon. Add the water, squash, lentils, red bell peppers, and celery. Simmer uncovered until the lentils are tender, about 30 minutes.

Stir in the spinach, cilantro, currants, Bragg Liquid Aminos, vinegar, salt to taste, and cayenne and let simmer just long enough for the spinach to wilt.

2 tablespoons ghee

1 small onion, finely chopped

1 tablespoon minced fresh ginger

1 clove garlic, minced

2 teaspoons ground cumin

2 teaspoons paprika

2 teaspoons ground coriander

1 teaspoon ground cinnamon

5 cups water

2 cups peeled and diced butternut squash

1 cup dried red lentils

1 cup diced red bell peppers

1 stalk celery, thinly sliced

1 bunch of fresh spinach, washed, stemmed, and finely chopped

1/2 cup chopped fresh cilantro

1/4 cup currants or chopped pitted dates

3 tablespoons Bragg Liquid Aminos or natural soy sauce

1 teaspoon balsamic vinegar or apple cider vinegar

1 to 2 teaspoons salt

1/4 teaspoon cayenne

Portuguese White Bean and Kale Stew

This lovely, saffron-scented stew is complemented by fresh garden greens.

1 cup dried white beans, soaked in water overnight, or 1 (15-ounce) can organic white beans

5 cups vegetable stock or water

1 tablespoon sunflower oil

1 medium onion, chopped

1 clove garlic, minced

1/2 teaspoon whole fennel seeds

1/2 cup peeled and chopped potatoes

1/2 cup peeled and chopped parsnips

2 tablespoons minced fresh oregano, or 1 teaspoon dried oregano

2 bay leaves

1 tablespoon paprika

1/8 teaspoon saffron threads

2 red bell peppers, roasted (see page 68), peeled, and puréed, or 1 (8-ounce) jar roasted red peppers, seeded and puréed

1 cup stemmed and finely chopped kale

1/4 cup chopped fresh parsley

2 teaspoons salt

1 teaspoon ground coriander

1/2 teaspoon pepper

Rinse the soaked beans and place them in a soup pot with the vegetable stock or fresh water. Bring to a boil, cover, reduce the heat to medium, and simmer for 1 hour or until the beans are tender. (Note: If you are using larger dried white beans, such as lima beans, they could take up to 2 hours to cook.)

Heat the oil in another soup pot. Add the onions and garlic and sauté until tender, about 10 minutes. Add the fennel seeds and brown them lightly. Stir in the potatoes, parsnips, oregano, bay leaves, paprika, and saffron. Add the cooked beans along with their cooking water and simmer until the vegetables are tender. If you are using canned beans, add them along with the 5 cups vegetable stock or water now.

Stir in the puréed red peppers, kale, parsley, salt, coriander, and pepper and simmer another 10 minutes or until the kale is tender.

Time-Saver Method for Cooking Beans Using a Pressure Cooker

Shoshoni is at an 8,500-foot elevation, which is quite high. We can cook beans all day and they still may not get tender. Generally we use a pressure cooker to speed the cooking time.

Beans double or triple in size when cooked. Don't fill your pressure cooker more than one-quarter full with beans. Use double the amount of water or stock to beans.

Cooking beans in a pressure cooker takes about one-third the time it would take to cook them in an open pot. Follow the manufacturer's instructions for time and quantity. At Shoshoni it takes about forty-five to sixty minutes to cook beans in a pressure cooker. At lower elevations, beans take about thirty to forty-five minutes, depending on the type of bean.

Always cool the pressure cooker under cold water to release steam and pressure before opening it. If your beans aren't quite tender, reseal the pressure cooker and cook them a little longer. Use pressure-cooked beans just as you would any other cooked beans.

Thai Vegetable Curry

Serves 6 to 8

6 cups water

4 stalks fresh lemongrass, cut in 1-inch lengths, or ½ cup dried lemongrass

2 tablespoons ghee

1 onion, finely chopped

1 tablespoon minced fresh ginger

1 hot green chili, seeded and minced

1 teaspoon turmeric

1 teaspoon mild Thai curry paste (optional)

1 clove garlic, minced

½ cup peeled and cubed sweet potatoes

½ cup peeled and cubed white potatoes

¼ cup sliced carrots

¼ cup coarsely chopped red bell peppers

2 cups coconut milk

¼ cup sliced yellow squash (cut in half lengthwise before slicing)

¼ cup broccoli florets

¼ cup fresh or frozen green peas

½ cup minced fresh basil

2 tablespoons Sucanat or other natural sugar

2 teaspoons salt

This soup is a staple at Shoshoni. It is so delicious and pleasing to the eye as well. We always serve Thai curry with simple basmati rice on the side.

Bring the water to a boil in a large pot. Add the lemongrass, cover, and simmer on low for 10 minutes. Set aside.

Heat the ghee in a separate large pot. Add the onion and sauté until lightly browned. Stir in the ginger, chili, turmeric, optional curry paste, and garlic and sauté for 5 minutes. Add the sweet potatoes, white potatoes, carrots, red bell peppers, and reserved lemongrass broth. Bring to a boil, reduce the heat, cover, and simmer until the vegetables are tender. Stir in the coconut milk, squash, broccoli, and green peas and cook for 10 to 15 minutes, or until the vegetables are tender but still retain their color. Stir in the basil, Sucanat, and salt.

Vietnamese Vegetable Rice Noodle Bowl

1 tablespoon toasted sesame oil

1/2 medium onion, sliced in half-moons

1/4 cup peeled and thinly sliced fresh ginger

6 cups vegetable stock or water

1 cup stemmed and sliced fresh shiitake mushrooms

1 tablespoon vegetable broth powder

1 tablespoon Bragg Liquid Aminos or natural soy sauce

1/2 teaspoon ground star anise

1/2 teaspoon salt

1 cup finely chopped bok choy

12 ounces rice noodles

Toppings

2 cups mung bean sprouts

1 cup shredded napa cabbage

1 cup chopped fresh basil leaves

1/2 cup cubed firm tofu marinated in 1/4 cup natural soy sauce

1/3 cup thinly sliced scallions

1/3 cup chopped fresh cilantro

1 green chili, seeded and thinly sliced

This soup makes a nice presentation for dinner guests or a fun change for a family meal. It is fun to set all of the toppings in small bowls in the middle of the table and then serve the noodles and soup broth and let everyone garnish their bowls as desired.

Heat the sesame oil in a large soup pot. Add the onion and ginger and sauté for 2 minutes. Stir in the vegetable stock, mushrooms, broth powder, Bragg Liquid Aminos, star anise, and salt. Cover and simmer for 30 minutes. Add the bok choy and simmer uncovered for 5 to 10 minutes.

Meanwhile, boil the rice noodles in water for about 3 minutes. Rinse in cold water, drain, and keep at room temperature.

Place the rice noodles in large, individual soup bowls using about 1 cup of noodles per bowl. Ladle some of the soup broth over the noodles. Garnish each bowl with an assortment of the toppings or arrange the toppings in small bowls on the serving table and allow people to top their own.

Pumpkin and Lentil Soup with Fresh Fennel

Serves 4 to 6

Here is a simple lentil stew infused with the flavor of fresh fennel.

1 small bulb fresh fennel

1/4 cup extra-virgin olive oil

1 onion, finely chopped

4 cups vegetable stock or water

1 cup dried lentils, rinsed and
   drained

1 tablespoon whole fennel seeds

1/2 pound peeled and chunked
   pumpkin (butternut or acorn
   squash can be substituted if
   pumpkin is not available)

Salt and pepper

Clean the fennel by cutting away the stalks and removing any brown parts. Chop the feathery green leaves into 1-inch pieces and set aside. Chop the fennel bulb coarsely.

Heat the oil in a heavy-bottomed soup pot. Add the onion and sauté until golden, about 10 minutes. Stir in the chopped fennel bulb and sauté 5 minutes. Add the vegetable stock, lentils, and fennel seeds. Bring to a boil, reduce the heat, and simmer uncovered for 30 minutes or until the lentils are partly tender. Add the pumpkin and simmer uncovered another 30 minutes or until the pumpkin chunks and lentils are tender. Season with salt and pepper to taste. Serve in individual bowls garnished with the chopped fennel greens.

Main Course Dishes

Autumn Vegetable Cobbler

Casserole Filling

1 large butternut squash (about 1 pound)

1 tablespoon ghee

$1/2$ small onion, minced

1 cup thinly sliced fresh shiitake
   mushrooms

1 cup trimmed and sliced green beans
   (in 1-inch lengths)

1 carrot, peeled and diced

1 small parsnip, peeled and diced

$1/2$ cup water

2 tablespoons arrowroot or cornstarch
   dissolved in $1/4$ cup cold water

8 ounces spinach, washed, stemmed, and
   chopped (about 4 cups)

2 tablespoons Bragg Liquid Aminos or
   natural soy sauce

1 tablespoon minced fresh sage, or
   1 teaspoon dried sage

2 teaspoons salt

$1/4$ teaspoon pepper

Biscuit Crust Mix

$1^{1/3}$ cups whole wheat pastry flour

$1^{1/2}$ teaspoons baking powder

$1/2$ teaspoon salt

4 tablespoons chilled ghee or unsalted
   butter

$1/2$ cup ice cold milk or soymilk

Fresh, sweet autumn squash and vegetables topped with a biscuit crust warm up a cold fall day.

Cut the squash into quarters, scrape out the seeds, and steam until tender. While the squash is steaming, heat the ghee in a saucepan. Add the onions and sauté until translucent. Add the mushrooms and sauté until their natural juices begin to release. Add the green beans, carrot, and parsnip. Stir in the 1/2 cup of water, cover, and simmer until the vegetables are tender.

When the squash is tender, peel and discard the skin, place the flesh in a bowl, and whip it with an electric beater until creamy. Alternatively, mash the squash in a food processor until it is smooth and creamy. Stir the mashed squash into the pot with the cooked vegetables. Bring to a simmer and stir in the dissolved arrowroot. Simmer until slightly thickened, about 5 minutes. Stir in the spinach, Bragg Liquid Aminos, sage, salt, and pepper. Pour into a lightly oiled, deep, 8 x12-inch casserole dish and set aside.

Preheat the oven to 375°F. To prepare the crust, combine the flour, baking powder, and salt in a medium bowl. Using a pastry blender or two forks, work the ghee into the flour mixture a little at a time until it is well incorporated. Alternatively, fit a food processor with the pastry-cutting blade and blend the dry ingredients in the processor bowl. Add the ghee and process until it is well incorporated.

Pour the milk into a separate bowl and whisk in about 1/2 cup of the flour mixture. Stir in the remainder of the flour mixture and form the dough into a ball. Turn onto a lightly floured surface and roll out with a rolling pin. Fold in half and then in half again. Roll out into a circle about 1/4-inch thick.

Carefully lift the biscuit crust onto the casserole or cut the dough with a biscuit cutter and lay the biscuits on top of the filling. Bake the cobbler for 30 minutes or until browned on top.

Gingered Chickpeas with Squash and Peppers

Louki squash is a long, light green vegetable found in various sizes. It is common in Asian countries and has many different names. Louki is the Indian name. If you have trouble finding louki, you can substitute zucchini for a similar taste.

Heat 1 tablespoon of the ghee in a cast-iron skillet. When hot but not smoking, add the squash and pan-fry until brown and tender. Remove from the pan and set aside.

2 tablespoons ghee

2 cups peeled and cubed louki squash or cubed zucchini

1 1/2 tablespoons minced fresh ginger

2 hot green chilies, seeded and minced

1 1/2 teaspoons whole cumin seeds

1 tablespoon ground coriander

2 teaspoons paprika

1 teaspoon turmeric

1/4 teaspoon asafetida

2 cups cooked chickpeas

2 cups Roasted Red Pepper Sauce, page 68

1/2 cup water

1 pound fresh green chard, washed twice, stemmed, and coarsely chopped

1/2 cup minced fresh cilantro

1 1/2 teaspoons salt

1 teaspoon Garam Masala, page 70

Add the remaining 1 tablespoon of ghee to the skillet and heat. Add the ginger, chilies, and cumin seeds, and fry for about 1 minute. Stir in the coriander, paprika, turmeric, and asafetida and sauté just long enough to brown the spices lightly.

Stir in the chickpeas, Roasted Red Pepper Sauce, and water. Cover and simmer for 15 to 20 minutes. Five or ten minutes before serving, stir in the browned louki squash, chard, cilantro, salt, and Garam Masala. Simmer uncovered until the chard is tender.

Creamy Potatoes in Seasoned Coconut Milk

Swamiji loves good, nourishing, Ayurvedic dishes. This is one of his favorite recipes. It is simple yet flavorful. Serve with Young Japanese Eggplant and Cauliflower Curry, page 163, and Homemade Urad Dal Patties, page 22, for a feast.

Bring the water to a boil in a large pot. Add the potatoes and cook uncovered until tender, about 20 minutes. Drain.

3 cups water

4 white potatoes, peeled and cut into 1-inch chunks

1 tablespoon ghee

1/2 onion, minced

1 inch fresh ginger, minced

1/4 green chili, seeded and minced

1 teaspoon turmeric

1 teaspoon paprika

1 cup coconut milk

1/4 cup chopped fresh cilantro

1 teaspoon salt

Heat the ghee in a skillet. Add the onion, ginger, and chili and sauté for 5 minutes. Add the turmeric and paprika and sauté for 1 minute. Then stir in the potatoes and the coconut milk. Mix until heated and thick. Stir in the cilantro. Season with salt to taste.

Crisp Moo Shoo Vegetables

Serves 4 to 6

You don't have to go out for Moo Shoo anymore. This special Shoshoni variation has a lot of nutritious vegetables, and we like to use tofu instead of the traditional scrambled egg.

Moo Shoo Filling

2 tablespoons toasted sesame oil

1 cup julienned carrots

1 tablespoon minced fresh ginger

8 cups shredded bok choy

1 cup julienned zucchini

1 cup thinly sliced fresh shiitake mushrooms

2 tablespoons Bragg Liquid Aminos or natural soy sauce

1 cup crumbled firm tofu

1/2 teaspoon turmeric

Heat the oil in a wok or skillet. Add the carrots and ginger and sauté until almost tender. Stir in the bok choy, zucchini, mushrooms, and Bragg Liquid Aminos, and sauté 5 to 10 minutes or until the vegetables are bright green and slightly tender. Remove the vegetables from the pan and set aside.

Add the tofu and turmeric to the cooking juices left in the pan. Cook until the liquid evaporates and the tofu is an even yellow color. Mix the tofu into the vegetables. Wrap about 1/4 cup of the filling in each scallion pancake. Serve with Fresh Hoisin Sauce on the side.

with Homemade Scallion Pancakes

For a complete Moo Shoo menu, serve it with Stir Fried Rice with Whole Cashews, page 173, and our Fresh Hoisin Sauce, page 61.

Scallion Pancakes
(makes 12)

2 cups sifted, whole wheat pastry flour or unbleached white flour

$2/3$ to $3/4$ cups boiling water

1 tablespoon ghee, melted

$1/2$ cup chopped scallions

1 teaspoon salt

Place the flour in a medium bowl. Mix the water with the melted ghee and add to the flour along with the scallions. Stir and knead the dough until it is smooth. Roll the dough into a long rope and cut into 6 pieces.

Roll each piece into a ball, and each ball into a flat pancake. Brush one side of one pancake with a little oil and place another pancake on top of it. Roll them both as thinly as possible into a 6-inch-wide pancake. Cook on a hot, ungreased skillet. Turn as air bubbles appear on the surface and cook briefly on the other side. Remove from the heat and peel apart the two pancakes. (Do not overcook. Overcooking will result in a hard, cracker-like pancake.) Stack the pancakes and wrap them in a clean towel until ready to serve.

Curried Zucchini and Bell Peppers

This is an elegant entrée for any holiday when served with basmati rice and Toor Dal with Eggplant and Potatoes, page 80.

Heat the ghee in a saucepan until very hot. Add the mustard seeds and cover. Shake the pan (as when making popcorn) until the seeds begin to pop.

Curried Vegetables

2 tablespoons ghee

2 teaspoons whole black mustard seeds

1/2 onion, finely chopped

2 teaspoons whole cumin seeds

1 clove garlic, minced

6 cups diced zucchini

1 red bell pepper, diced

1 tablespoon paprika

1 teaspoon Garam Masala, page 70

1/2 teaspoon turmeric

1/4 cup chickpea flour

2 cups hot water

1/4 cup chopped fresh cilantro

2 teaspoons salt

Pinch of cayenne (optional)

Lower the heat and add the onion, cumin seeds, and garlic. Sauté for 1 minute. Add the zucchini, bell pepper, paprika, Garam Masala, and turmeric and sauté for 5 minutes.

Sprinkle the chickpea flour over the vegetables and stir to coat them. Gradually stir in the hot water, adding it slowly and stirring constantly to prevent lumping. Cover the pan and turn down the heat. Simmer gently for 15 to 20 minutes.

While the vegetables are cooking, heat 1 cup of canola oil in a skillet. Cut the cheese into bite-size cubes and fry it in the oil until brown all over. Drain on a paper towel and add the cheese to the vegetable stew. Season the stew with the cilantro, salt, and optional cayenne.

Note: For a vegan version of this recipe, use 1 pound firm tofu instead of the panir cheese. Fry it in oil as directed for the panir.

with Fresh Country-Style Panir Cheese

You will be surprised at how easy it is to make this country-style cheese.

Panir Cheese
(makes 1½ cups, about 12 ounces)

½ gallon whole milk

4 tablespoons fresh lime or lemon juice or white vinegar (fresh lime juice works best)

Pinch of salt

To make the cheese, pour the milk into a large pot and bring it to a boil over low to medium heat. When the milk has reached a rolling boil, stir in the lime juice. The milk will curdle and separate from the whey. Line a colander with cheesecloth, place the colander in a bowl, and carefully ladle the curdled milk into the lined colander. Wrap the curds tightly in the cloth, place in a bowl, and put a plate or weight on top of the cheese to squeeze out the remaining moisture. Place in the refrigerator for later use. Save the whey for cooking stock.

Fresh Spinach and Basil Pesto-Stuffed Shells

Serves 4 to 6

This delicious sauce combines the sweetness of carrots and beets with fresh garden herbs. It is warming and flavorful without the acidic taste and aftereffects of tomato sauce.

Pesto Filling

6 ounces (about 3 cups) fresh basil leaves

3 tablespoons walnuts

1/2 cup freshly grated Parmesan cheese (optional)

1/4 cup extra-virgin olive oil

1 clove garlic

4 ounces (about 2 cups) fresh spinach, cleaned, stemmed, and finely chopped

1/2 cup crumbled firm tofu or low-fat cottage cheese, drained

Salt

10 large pasta shells, cooked al dente and drained

Preheat the oven to 350°F. To make the Pesto Filling, combine the basil, walnuts, optional Parmesan cheese, olive oil, and garlic in a food processor and blend into a thick paste. Transfer to a bowl. Heat the spinach in a dry skillet and sauté until lightly cooked. Drain the cooking liquid from the spinach and add the spinach to the basil mixture along with the tofu or cottage cheese and salt to taste. Mix well and stuff each pasta shell with a generous amount of the filling.

To assemble, pour a layer of the sauce (about 1 cup) into the bottom of a shallow, 8 x 12-inch baking dish. Arrange the shells in the dish in a single layer and pour 3 cups of the sauce over the top. Cover and bake for 20 to 30 minutes, or just long enough to heat through. Garnish each serving with a ladle of Savory Red Sauce and a little fresh Parmesan cheese, if desired.

with *Savory Red Sauce*

Enjoy this sauce as part of this recipe or as a substitute for tomato sauce in any Italian recipe.

To make the Savory Red Sauce, melt the ghee in a skillet. Add the carrots, onion, and garlic. Cover and sauté until tender, about 15 to 20 minutes.

Transfer to a blender or food processor fitted with a metal blade. Add the stock, beet, Bragg Liquid Aminos, rosemary, oregano, salt, and pepper and purée into a thick, red sauce. You may need to process the sauce in batches depending on the size of your blender or food processor.

Savory Red Sauce
(makes 6 cups)

2 tablespoons ghee, melted

4 cups peeled and diced carrots (about 2 pounds)

1/2 large onion, minced

2 cloves garlic, minced

3 cups vegetable stock or water

1 small beet, peeled, chopped and boiled until tender, or 1 cup diced canned beets

2 tablespoons Bragg Liquid Aminos or natural soy sauce

1 tablespoon minced fresh rosemary, or 1 teaspoon dried rosemary

1 tablespoon minced fresh oregano, or 1 teaspoon dried oregano

2 teaspoons salt

1/2 teaspoon pepper

Grilled Indian Spiced Potatoes

Enjoy these home-fried potatoes alongside any curry or dal soup or serve them for a spicy breakfast.

Steam the potatoes until tender and set aside. Heat the ghee in a large, cast-iron skillet until hot but not smoking. Add the mustard seeds and cook until they turn gray and start to pop. Stir in the onions, ginger, and green chili and sauté for 5 minutes.

Stir in the green bell pepper and the Pitta Spice and sauté for 1 minute. Add the reserved potatoes and fry until crispy on the outside. Season with the salt and a pinch of pepper.

2 large russet potatoes, peeled and cut in 1-inch chunks

1 tablespoon ghee

1/2 teaspoon whole black mustard seeds

1 cup coarsely chopped onions

1-inch piece of fresh ginger, minced

1/2 green chili, seeded and minced

1/2 green bell pepper, coarsely chopped

1/2 teaspoon Pitta Spice, page 72

1/2 teaspoon salt

Pinch of pepper

Italian Zucchini Pancakes

Swami's Italian mother, Mama Putorti, taught Faith this simple, very tasty dish. Zucchini pancakes are wonderful served as a side dish. They also make a light dinner and are especially good served with Italian beans.

Grate the zucchini into a bowl and sprinkle it lightly with salt. Wait about 10 minutes or until the zucchini sweats, then squeeze off the excess moisture.

1 pound fresh zucchini

1 cup unbleached white or whole wheat pastry flour

2 eggs, lightly beaten

1 tablespoon minced fresh basil, or 1/2 teaspoon dried basil

Salt and pepper

Pinch of cayenne

Olive oil for pan-frying

Freshly grated Romano or Parmesan cheese (optional)

Transfer the zucchini to a large bowl and stir in the flour, eggs, basil, and salt, pepper, and cayenne to taste. Add a little more flour if the batter seems too loose. Coat the bottom of a heavy skillet with olive oil. Heat the oil until hot but not smoking. Drop the zucchini batter from a serving spoon, using about 1/4 cup batter per pancake, and gently press it out with the back of the spoon. Fry until browned on both sides. Split one in half to check that it's not gooey in the center. Transfer the cooked pancakes to paper towels to absorb excess oil. Serve hot, warm, or chilled, with a sprinkle of freshly grated cheese, if desired.

Lasagne Primavera with Whole Wheat Noodles

Serves 8 to 10

Our vegetable stuffed lasagna includes whole wheat noodles for extra flavor and nutrition. This savory dish uses a tomato-free sauce for a unique and distinctive flavor. However, you can substitute your favorite tomato sauce to save time or for a more traditional taste.

2 tablespoons olive oil

2 cloves garlic, minced

1 onion, finely chopped

2 yellow summer squash or zucchini, thinly sliced (about 3 cups)

1 red bell pepper, seeded and diced

4 ounces (about 2 cups) fresh spinach, washed, stemmed, and chopped

2 cups ricotta or cottage cheese or Tofu Ricotta, page 66

1/2 pound grated mozzarella cheese or soy cheese (about 2 cups)

1 cup (about 2 ounces) finely chopped fresh basil

3 tablespoons minced fresh chives (optional)

1/4 teaspoon pepper

6 cups Savory Red Sauce, page 109

1 (8-ounce) package whole wheat lasagna noodles (about 12 noodles)

1/2 cup (2 ounces) finely chopped fresh parsley

Preheat the oven to 350°F. Heat the oil in a skillet. Add the garlic and brown it lightly; add the onion and sauté until translucent. Stir in the squash and red bell pepper and sauté until tender, about 10 minutes. Remove the vegetables from the pan and set aside. Add the chopped spinach to the skillet and cook in the water that clings to the leaves until just wilted. Drain and add to the other vegetables.

Combine the ricotta cheese with 1 cup of the grated mozzarella, basil, chives, and pepper in a bowl and set aside.

Pour a layer of Savory Red Sauce (about 1 cup) over the bottom of a deep, 8 x 12-inch glass baking dish. Line the bottom of the dish with 4 uncooked lasagna noodles, 3 lengthwise and one across the top. Spread another 1 cup of sauce over the uncooked noodles. Arrange $1/3$ of the cooked vegetables (about 1 cup) on top of the noodles. Then, dollop $1/3$ of the cheese mixture (about 1 cup) over the vegetables. Arrange another layer of 4 noodles over the cheese mixture and repeat with sauce, vegetables, and cheese until the casserole is three layers deep with noodles, sauce, vegetables, and cheese. Be sure the top layer of noodles is well covered with sauce to ensure that they get as tender as the lower layers. You will need about $4^{1}/_{2}$ cups of Savory Red sauce to assemble the lasagne. This will leave $1^{1}/_{2}$ cups to spoon over the lasagne when it is served.

Cover and bake for 1 hour and 15 minutes. Uncover and sprinkle the remaining 1 cup of grated mozzarella cheese over the top of the casserole. Return to the oven for about 10 minutes to brown the cheese. Remove from the oven and let rest for 10 minutes. Cut the lasagne into 8 or 10 servings. Spoon a little sauce over the top of each serving and garnish with the parsley.

Matar Panir (green peas with homemade cheese)

Serves 6 to 8

This dish is an Indian classic. If you are in a hurry, substitute cubed tofu for the homemade cheese for a delicious variation.

1½ cups (12 ounces) Panir Cheese, page 107, pan-fried in oil until golden

2 tablespoons ghee

½ teaspoon whole black mustard seeds

2 teaspoons whole cumin seeds

¼ teaspoon whole fennel seeds

1 tablespoon minced fresh ginger

1 tablespoon ground coriander

1 hot green chili, seeded and minced (optional)

1½ teaspoons paprika

1 teaspoon turmeric

2 cups diced fresh tomatoes

1 cup whey (broth reserved from making panir) or water

2 cups fresh or frozen green peas

1 cup low-fat sour cream

2 tablespoons minced fresh cilantro

2 teaspoons Garam Masala, page 70

Salt

Heat the ghee in a heavy-bottomed saucepan until very hot. Add the mustard seeds and fry until they begin to pop and turn gray. Add the cumin and fennel seeds, stirring constantly.

Lower the heat and add the ginger, coriander, optional green chili, paprika, and turmeric. Stir to brown lightly and form a masala paste. Stir in the tomatoes and continue to cook until the tomatoes are tender, about 10 minutes.

Add the whey and the green peas and simmer over low heat until the peas are tender. Stir in the fried cheese.

Just before serving, stir in the sour cream, cilantro, Garam Masala, and salt to taste. Heat very gently and serve.

Saag Panir (spinach with homemade cheese)

Serves 6 to 8

This dish includes fresh spinach cooked until just tender and mixed with country-style cheese and fragrant spices. It has been a staple on the Sunday Indian Feast menu at Shoshoni for years.

1 jalapeno pepper, seeded and minced

1 teaspoon minced fresh ginger

1/2 teaspoon ground cumin

1/2 teaspoon ground coriander

1/2 teaspoon ground turmeric

1/4 teaspoon paprika

6 tablespoons ghee or vegetable oil

1 1/2 cups (12 ounces) Panir Cheese, page 107, cut into cubes

1 pound (8 cups) fresh spinach, washed, trimmed, and chopped

1/2 cup cream

1/2 teaspoon Garam Masala, page 70

Salt

Combine the jalapeno pepper, ginger, and 4 tablespoons of water in a blender or food processor and blend into a smooth purée. Add the cumin, coriander, turmeric, and paprika and pulse to blend well. Set aside.

Heat the ghee in a cast-iron or nonstick skillet. Add the panir and fry until it is browned on all sides. Drain on paper towels.

Using the same pan and oil, carefully add the puréed spices; then gradually stir in the chopped spinach. Reduce the heat, cover, and cook until the spinach is wilted, about 5 minutes. Stir in the panir, cream, Garam Masala, and salt to taste and simmer for 10 minutes over low heat so the flavors can blend. Serve hot.

Pumpkin Gnocchi

Serves 6

Homemade pasta dumplings smothered in an earthy pumpkin sauce are delectable. Faith invented this dish to make use of the abundance of pumpkins in the fall.

Steam the pumpkin until very tender, about 10 to 15 minutes. Remove 2 cups of the pumpkin chunks and set aside. Mash the remaining 6 cups of pumpkin. Stir in the egg and olive oil. Then stir in the flours and salt and pepper to taste. Mix until the dough is smooth and does not stick to the sides of the bowl. Chill the dough until ready to use.

Bring a large pot of salted water to a boil (use about 8 cups of water with ¹/₂ teaspoon salt added). To shape the gnocchi, fill a tablespoon with some of the pumpkin dough. With your thumb press a small amount of dough over the end of the spoon and pinch off by pressing your thumb against the spoon. If you like, you can form small crescent shapes by pressing the dough over the side of the spoon. One spoonful will make 3 or 4 gnocchis. You can drop them onto a floured baking sheet to be cooked later or drop them directly into the boiling water.

Add about 6 gnocchi to the water at a time. Cook until they are swollen and floating on the surface, about 2 or 3 minutes. Drain the gnocchi in a strainer and place them in a bowl with a little olive oil to prevent them from sticking to each other or to the bowl. Finish cooking the remaining gnocchi in the same fashion.

Pumpkin Gnocchi

8 cups chunked raw pumpkin removed from shell (about one 2-pound pumpkin)

1 egg

2 tablespoons olive oil

2¹/₂ cups whole wheat pastry flour

2¹/₂ cups unbleached white flour

Salt and pepper

with Pumpkin Mushroom Sauce

Pumpkin Mushroom Sauce

$1/4$ cup olive oil

1 onion, cut in half and thinly sliced

1 bell pepper (green, red, or yellow), cut in half, seeded, and thinly sliced

3 cloves garlic, finely chopped

1 cup sliced button or chanterelle mushrooms

2 cups steamed pumpkin (reserved from the gnocchi)

Salt and pepper

To Serve

2 tablespoons chopped fresh basil

1 cup (about 4 ounces) freshly grated Parmesan cheese or sharp soy cheese

Heat the olive oil in a skillet. Add the onion, bell pepper, and garlic and sauté until just tender. Add the mushrooms and sauté for another minute or two or until they are tender. Purée the steamed pumpkin in a blender or food processor and stir into the sautéed onion mixture. Season with salt and pepper to taste.

Toss the cooked gnocchi with the Pumpkin Mushroom Sauce and the chopped fresh basil. Sprinkle the top with the freshly grated cheese and serve.

Spinach Fettuccine with Almond Basil Sauce

Fettuccine Alfredo was one of Shanti's favorite Italian dishes while growing up. She created a healthy cream-free alternative that is every bit as delicious.

2 tablespoons ghee

1 clove garlic, minced

2 cups blanched almonds, soaked in water to cover for at least 4 hours and drained

1/2 onion, minced

2 tablespoons whole wheat pastry flour

4 cups milk or plain soymilk

1/2 pound asparagus

1/2 small red bell pepper, seeded and sliced

2 teaspoons salt

1/4 teaspoon pepper

8 ounces spinach fettuccine noodles

1/2 cup chopped fresh basil

Heat the ghee in a medium saucepan. Add the garlic and sauté until lightly browned. Add the almonds and onion and sauté for about 5 minutes. Add the flour, sprinkling in a little at a time and whisking to coat the nuts and onion. Gradually whisk in the milk, stirring constantly to avoid lumps. Season with the salt and pepper. Cook over low heat, stirring occasionally, until thickened, about 10 minutes.

Ladle the sauce into a blender and purée until very smooth. Pour the sauce back into the pot and simmer gently.

Cook the noodles in boiling water until al dente. Drain well.

Snap off and discard the tough ends of the asparagus. Steam the whole asparagus stalks and sliced bell pepper until tender but slightly crunchy, about 5 minutes. Pour the warm sauce over the fettuccine and top with the steamed vegetables and chopped fresh basil. Toss gently and serve.

Sunny Yellow Squash and Tofu Quiche

Serves 4 to 6

Here's a light and delicious way to brighten up a brunch menu. Serve it with Fresh Herb and Baby Greens Salad, page 30.

Preheat the oven to 350°F. Prebake the pie crust for 10 minutes and let cool. Heat the oil in a skillet and sauté the onion and garlic until translucent.

Add the squash, raise the heat, and sauté for 5 minutes or until tender. Set aside.

Combine one-half of the tofu along with the water, lemon juice, olive oil, tahini, salt, pepper, turmeric, and nutmeg in a food processor and blend until smooth and creamy. Cube the remaining tofu by hand and gently stir it in.

Fold the cooked vegetables and roasted red pepper into the tofu mixture. Spoon into the pie shell and bake for 1 hour or until the tofu has set. Remove from the oven and let rest for 10 minutes before serving. Garnish with a little paprika and the chopped parsley.

1 unbaked 9-inch pie crust (use our Basic Pastry Crust, page 229, or your favorite recipe)

1 tablespoon olive oil

1 small onion, minced

1 clove garlic, minced

2 cups diced yellow squash or zucchini or a mixture of both

12 ounces firm tofu

1/4 cup water

2 tablespoons fresh lemon juice

2 tablespoons olive oil

2 tablespoons tahini

2 teaspoons salt

1/4 teaspoon pepper

1/4 teaspoon turmeric

1/4 teaspoon grated nutmeg

1/2 cup roasted red bell peppers, or 1 (4-ounce) jar roasted red peppers, seeded and chopped

Paprika

1/4 cup chopped fresh parsley

Summer Squash and Grilled Bell Pepper Torte

Serves 6

This layered vegetable torte is like lasagne without the noodles. It's a delicious way to enjoy the bounty of zucchini and peppers in summertime.

Torte

1/4 cup olive oil

1 medium zucchini, sliced lengthwise into long, flat, 1/4-inch-thick strips

1 medium yellow squash, sliced lengthwise into long, flat, 1/4-inch-thick strips

1/2 red bell pepper, seeded and thinly sliced

1/2 yellow bell pepper, seeded and thinly sliced

1 cup ricotta cheese

1/2 teaspoon salt

A few pinches of pepper

3 tablespoons chopped fresh parsley or basil or a mixture of both

Cover the bottom of a cast-iron skillet or griddle with a thin layer of olive oil. Heat over high and sear the zucchini and squash until almost cooked. Remove the zucchini and squash and sear the bell pepper slices. Season with the salt and pepper.

Cover the bottom of a 9 x 13-inch baking pan with a thin layer of the prepared sauce. Arrange a layer of half of the zucchini, squash, and peppers over the sauce, and spoon half of the ricotta over the vegetables. Repeat with another layer of the remaining zucchini, squash, peppers, and ricotta. Pour the remaining sauce over the top.

Cover and bake for 30 to 40 minutes. Remove the cover and bake 5 to 10 minutes longer. Garnish the casserole with the fresh parsley or basil.

with Ricotta Cheese

Place the water in a large saucepan and bring to a boil. Add the carrots and simmer uncovered for about 10 minutes or until tender. Drain well.

Sauce

6 cups water

4 cups chopped carrots

3 tablespoons olive oil

2 pounds ripe tomatoes

$\frac{1}{4}$ onion, coarsely chopped

2 cloves garlic, minced

1 cup finely chopped fresh basil

Salt and pepper

Preheat the oven to 350°F. Heat the olive oil in a heavy-bottomed skillet and sear the tomatoes whole until the skins are charred and blistered. Transfer to a food processor or blender and purée the tomatoes with the cooked carrots until smooth. Set aside.

In the same skillet, sauté the onion and garlic until soft. Pour the puréed carrots and tomatoes into the pan along with the fresh basil and salt and pepper to taste. Cover and simmer on low for 15 minutes.

Swamiji's Favorite Potato Pancakes
with Roasted Red Peppers

Serves 4

These crispy pan-fried potato patties are a spicy alternative to traditional potato pancakes. Enjoy them with Warming Whole Mung Dal, page 81 and Spicy Masala Green Beans, page 159.

Heat the oil in a cast-iron skillet. Add the mustard seeds and fry until they turn gray and pop. Quickly add the urad dal and sauté until browned.

1 teaspoon sunflower oil

1/2 teaspoon whole black mustard seeds

1 teaspoon urad dal

1/2 teaspoon whole cumin seeds

1/2 teaspoon turmeric

1/4 teaspoon dried fenugreek leaves or dried basil

4 medium russet potatoes, peeled and grated

1/2 cup roasted red pepper slices

Salt

1 tablespoon plain yogurt

Stir in the cumin seeds, turmeric, and fenugreek leaves. Then stir in the grated potatoes. Pat the potatoes over the bottom of the pan. Scatter the roasted red pepper slices over the top. Fry until the bottom is crispy, adding more oil as necessary. Flip the potatoes over like a pancake and fry the other side. Season with salt to taste. Serve with a tablespoon of yogurt on top.

Tomato Flan

This dish is an old favorite. Faith began making it at Rudi's Restaurant in Boulder, Colorado. It's a delicious, Italian-style quiche seasoned with fresh basil and Parmesan cheese.

Preheat the oven to 350°F. Prebake the pie crust for 5 minutes or until lightly browned. Remove from the oven and let cool.

1 unbaked 9-inch pie crust (use our Basic Pastry Crust, page 229, or your favorite recipe)

2 tablespoons olive oil

1 onion, sliced in half-moons

2 cloves garlic, minced

4 medium zucchinis, sliced

4 tomatoes, wedged

3 eggs

1/4 cup minced fresh basil, or 2 tablespoons dried basil

1/2 teaspoon salt

A pinch of pepper

A few dashes of Tabasco

1/2 cup freshly grated Parmesan cheese

Heat the oil in a skillet. Add the onion and garlic and sauté until translucent. Add the zucchini and tomatoes and sauté until barely tender, about 10 minutes. Season with salt, pepper, and Tabasco to taste.

Drain and reserve the juice from the sautéed vegetables. Beat 2 of the eggs and stir into the drained vegetable juice along with the basil. Stir this mixture into the vegetables and pour into the prebaked pie crust. Beat the remaining egg with the Parmesan cheese and pour over the top of the pie. Bake at 350°F for about 45 minutes or until the egg topping is browned and firm.

Udon Noodles with Grilled Tofu and Mandarin Sauce

Don't you love one-pot meals? This noodle dish is great on its own or can be enjoyed as part of an Asian feast.

S lice the tofu lengthwise into two squares or slabs. Heat 1 tablespoon of the sesame oil in a heavy skillet and fry the tofu on both sides until golden. Remove the tofu from the skillet, cube, and set aside.

Add the remaining oil to the skillet and sauté the carrots for 5 minutes. Add the mushrooms and sauté until they begin to soften. Add the peas, optional bamboo shoots, bell peppers, and mung bean sprouts and sauté over high heat until just tender, about 5 minutes.

Meanwhile, combine the tahini, orange juice, soy sauce, and hot chili oil in a blender and process into a smooth sauce. Alternatively, whisk in a bowl until smooth.

Add the cooked noodles and fried tofu to the vegetables and pour the sauce over the top. Toss gently to combine. Stir-fry over high heat briefly and serve hot, garnished with the scallions.

½ pound firm tofu

2 tablespoons toasted sesame oil

1 cup sliced fresh shiitake mushrooms

1 cup julienned carrots

½ cup fresh or frozen green peas

½ cup bamboo shoots (optional)

½ cup thinly sliced red bell peppers

½ cup mung bean sprouts

½ cup tahini

½ cup freshly squeezed orange juice

¼ cup natural soy sauce

Dash of hot chili oil (optional)

6 ounces udon noodles, cooked and drained

¼ cup thinly sliced scallions

Yoga Kitchen

Specialties

Special Occasion Dishes

Easy Dinners and Picnic Favorites

Acorn Squash Baked in Cashew Sauce

Serves 4 to 6

This casserole is like a rich gratin without all the cheese and cream. It is very satisfying as a main dish accompanied by Steamed Kale with Sliced Dates and Toasted Pecans, page 161.

2 medium acorn squash (about 2 pounds total)

2 tablespoons ghee

1 onion, finely chopped

2 teaspoons dried sage

2 cups raw cashews

2 cups vegetable stock or water

2 teaspoons salt

Pepper

1/2 cup coarse dried bread crumbs (optional)

1/4 cup chopped fresh parsley

Preheat the oven to 350°F. Lightly oil a deep, 8 x 12-inch casserole dish.

Cut each squash into quarters. Scrape out the seeds and place in a steamer basket in a large saucepan. Steam until fork tender. Let the squash cool before handling, then peel and discard the skins and cut into 1- or 2-inch cubes. Transfer to the prepared casserole dish and set aside.

Heat the ghee in a cast-iron skillet. Add the onion and sauté until soft. Sprinkle in the sage and stir to coat the onion.

While the onion is cooking, combine the cashews and stock in a blender and process until smooth and creamy. Season with salt and pepper. Pour over the onions and stir until well combined. Let simmer gently for a few minutes, just enough for the flavors to blend, and remove from the heat. Pour evenly over the cooked squash. Cover and bake for 20 to 30 minutes. Uncover, sprinkle the optional bread crumbs over the top, and return to the oven to brown for 5 to 10 minutes. Garnish with the parsley.

Aubergines Farcis

This dish consists of tender eggplant slices wrapped around fresh, steamed asparagus. It's a delightful contrast between the softness of eggplant and the crispness of lightly cooked, fresh spring asparagus. It was inspired by Faith's love of these two wonderful vegetables.

Snap off and discard the tough ends of the asparagus. Steam the whole asparagus stalks until bright green and only slightly tender, about 1 or 2 minutes. Set aside.

2 bunches (about 1 pound) of fresh asparagus

2 ripe eggplants, peeled and cut lengthwise into 1/4-inch slices

1 cup unbleached white flour

2 tablespoons Romano cheese (optional)

1 teaspoon dried basil

1/2 teaspoon dried rosemary

Pinch of salt and pepper

Olive oil

1/2 pound Gruyère cheese, grated

Lightly salt the eggplant slices and place on paper towels to sweat (this removes any bitterness and excess moisture from the eggplant). After 10 minutes wipe off the excess moisture.

Combine the flour with the optional Romano cheese, basil, rosemary, salt, and pepper. Mix well. Lightly coat a cast-iron skillet or sauté pan with olive oil and heat it over medium-high. Dredge the eggplant slices in the seasoned flour and fry them in the skillet until browned on both sides. Add more olive oil as needed when the slices have absorbed all that is in the pan. Drain the slices on paper towels to remove excess oil.

Preheat the oven to 350°F. Lightly oil a deep, 8 x 12-inch baking dish. Roll the asparagus spears lengthwise in the slices of browned eggplant and place them in the prepared baking dish. Top the stuffed eggplant with the grated Gruyere cheese and bake for 15 minutes or until heated through and the cheese is melted and bubbly.

Artichokes Florentine

Trim the artichokes, removing the stalks and tough outer leaves. Trim the barbs off the remaining leaves and trim the artichoke bottoms with a knife to make them smooth. Cover the bottom of a pot large enough to hold the artichokes in a single layer (or use two pots, if necessary) with a thin layer of oil and garlic and heat over medium-high. Place the artichokes, bottom-side down, in the pan and brown the bottoms. Invert the artichokes (bottoms up) and fill the pot with stock or water up to the base of the leaves. Cover the artichoke bottoms with wine and more water as needed. Place a heavy plate over the artichokes to keep them from floating up and flipping over as they cook.

Cover the pot and bring to a boil. Reduce the heat and simmer for about 45 minutes or until a leaf pulls away easily and is tender.

Combine the butter and flour in a saucepan to make a roux (thick paste). Rapidly whisk in the steaming milk. Heat over medium until thickened, whisking briskly and constantly to prevent lumps. Gently whisk in the Swiss cheese, nutmeg, and salt and pepper to taste. Cover, remove from the heat, and set aside.

The Artichokes

6 fresh artichokes

4 tablespoons olive oil

3 cloves garlic, minced

6 to 8 cups vegetable stock or water

2 cups white wine (non-alcoholic wine is fine, or omit)

Mornay Sauce

2½ tablespoons melted butter

2 tablespoons unbleached white flour

1½ cups steaming hot milk or plain soymilk

1 cup (4 ounces) grated Swiss cheese or soy cheese

Pinch of grated nutmeg

Salt and pepper

This is a lovely addition to any holiday menu.

Wash the fresh spinach and remove the tough stems. Cook in the water that clings to the leaves until just wilted, about 5 minutes. Refresh under cold water, squeeze out the excess moisture, and chop. Stir the chopped spinach, grated cheddar, Romano, Tabasco, and pepper into the hot Mornay sauce.

Florentine

1 pound (about 8 cups) fresh spinach, or 2 cups chopped cooked spinach

1 cup (4 ounces) grated cheddar, Gruyère, or Swiss cheese (soy cheese may be substituted)

1 tablespoon grated Romano or soy cheese

1/4 teaspoon pepper

Dash of Tabasco or a pinch of cayenne

To Assemble

Gently spread the leaves of the artichokes to remove the fuzzy thistles with a spoon but do not flatten the leaves. Take care not to remove the fleshy artichoke heart. Fill the bowl-shaped opening with the spinach florentine. Serve with dipping butter for the artichoke, if desired.

Champignons Eleganté

To make the frangipane, combine the flour, egg yolks, nutmeg, and pepper in food processor. Process until the flour and yolks are thoroughly combined and the mixture resembles wet sand, about 10 seconds.

Frangipane

1/2 cup unbleached white flour

3 egg yolks

1 1/2 tablespoons butter, melted

Pinch of grated nutmeg

Pinch of pepper

1/2 cup scalded milk, hot

With the food processor running, drizzle in the melted butter and process until it is absorbed. With the machine still running, add the milk in a steady stream. Process until the mixture is thick, completely smooth, and pale yellow.

Transfer the frangipane to a skillet and cook over medium heat. Stir constantly until lumps begin to form. Continue stirring until the mixture forms a thick mass and leaves the sides of the pan, forming a thin film on the bottom of the pan. Reduce the heat to low. Continue stirring until the mixture turns waxy yellow, about 3 minutes.

Transfer the mixture to a flat plate and press into a thick pancake. Cover and refrigerate until completely chilled, about 2 hours or overnight.

Faith created this dish for Rudi's Restaurant in Boulder, Colorado. It is a rich, dairy-lover's concoction.

$\mathcal{T}$o make the champignons, wipe the mushrooms with a damp towel. Remove the stems and discard or reserve them for another use. Heat 3 tablespoons of the butter in a skillet. Add the mushroom caps and sauté until barely cooked. Remove from the skillet. Heat the remaining 3 tablespoons of butter in the skillet. Add the onions, celery, and garlic and sauté until tender.

Chop the chilled frangipane into small chunks. Place it in a bowl along with the sautéed onion mixture, Brie, almonds, dill, chervil, Tabasco, and salt and pepper to taste. Mix thoroughly.

Preheat the oven to 375°F. Fill the reserved mushroom caps with the frangipane mixture and chill them in the refrigerator for about 20 minutes to set. Bake for 20 to 30 minutes or until browned. Serve hot.

Champignons

3 pounds mushrooms (button mushrooms or shiitake mushrooms work well)

6 tablespoons butter

1/4 cup minced onions

1 stalk celery, thinly sliced

2 cloves garlic, minced

1/2 pound Brie cheese, cut into small chunks

1/4 cup (1 ounce) toasted slivered almonds

1 tablespoon minced fresh dill, or 1/2 teaspoon dried dill

1 teaspoon chopped fresh chervil, or a pinch of dried chervil

1 or 2 dashes Tabasco or your favorite hot sauce

Salt and pepper

Savory, Stuffed, Sun-Ripened Tomatoes

Serves 4

Shanti can't resist this delicious and lovely way to enjoy fresh plump tomatoes in late summer and early fall.

4 ripe tomatoes

1 tablespoon olive oil

1/2 onion, minced

2 cloves garlic, minced

3 ounces (about 1/2 cup) toasted almonds, finely chopped

8 ounces (about 4 cups) fresh spinach, stems removed and finely chopped

3 tablespoons minced fresh parsley

1 cup fine dried bread crumbs

3 tablespoons grated Parmesan cheese

2 tablespoons minced fresh basil

1/2 teaspoon salt

Pepper

Preheat the oven to 375°F. Lightly oil a shallow, 8 x 12-inch casserole dish. Slice off the very top portion of the tomatoes. Scoop out the insides with a spoon and place in a bowl. Remove and discard the seeds from the tomato pulp and reserve the remainder. Arrange the hollow tomatoes in the prepared casserole dish and set aside.

Heat the olive oil in a cast-iron skillet. Add the onion and garlic and sauté until browned. Add the almonds and sauté for another minute. Stir in the spinach, parsley, and reserved tomato pulp and cook until the spinach is wilted. Stir in the bread crumbs, Parmesan cheese, basil, salt, and pepper to taste. Fill each tomato with a generous amount of the mixture. Bake for 25 to 30 minutes or until the filling is hot.

Frittura Deluzie

Faith's recipe for Italian "crazy fritters" is made with fresh spinach and cheese.

Wash the spinach and cook it briefly in just the water that clings to the leaves. Quickly refresh the leaves under cold water, squeeze out the excess moisture, and chop.

8 ounces (about 4 cups tightly packed) fresh spinach, stems removed (1 1/2 cups cooked and chopped)

3/4 cup ricotta cheese

1/4 cup fine dried bread crumbs

1 egg, lightly beaten

2 tablespoons grated Parmesan cheese

1 tablespoon chopped fresh basil, or 1 teaspoon dried basil

1/4 teaspoon pepper

2 dashes Tabasco

About 1 cup unbleached white or whole wheat flour for dredging

2 cups vegetable oil for frying

Place the spinach in a bowl and stir in the ricotta cheese, bread crumbs, egg, Parmesan cheese, basil, pepper, and Tabasco. Mix well. Roll into balls about the size of a walnut, moistening your hands occasionally to prevent the mixture from sticking. The mixture will make about 30 fritturas.

Heat the oil in a large, heavy skillet. Roll the balls in the flour and fry them, 2 or 3 at a time, in the hot oil. Drain on paper towels. Serve as is or on a bed of pasta with your favorite tomato sauce. Sprinkle with freshly grated Parmesan or Romano cheese, if desired.

Shiitake Mushrooms Stuffed with Wild Rice

This is a variation of our classic Wild Rice Stuffing recipe that is in The Shoshoni Cookbook. *It makes a lovely addition to your holiday menu or anytime.*

8 cups water

4 cups wild rice

1/4 cup olive oil

1 pound fresh shiitake mushrooms, or 2 to 3 large mushrooms per person

1 cup minced onions

4 cloves fresh garlic, minced

1/4 cup minced fresh parsley

1 tablespoon dried rosemary

1 tablespoon dried thyme

1 tablespoon dried sage

1 tablespoon salt

1 teaspoon whole celery seeds

1/2 teaspoon pepper

1 cup leftover cornbread crumbs or coarse dried bread crumbs

2 ounces (about 1/4 cup) dried cherries

1 bunch of Swiss chard

2 tablespoons Bragg Liquid Aminos or natural soy sauce

on a Bed of Greens

Bring the water to a boil in a large saucepan. Add the wild rice and return to a boil. Lower the heat, cover, and simmer for 40 minutes. The rice is done when it is soft to the bite. Drain any excess water and set aside.

Generously oil a shallow, 8 x 12-inch baking dish. Clean the mushrooms with a damp paper towel and trim the stems. Heat 2 tablespoons of the oil in a skillet and lightly sauté the mushrooms until they are just partially cooked. Remove from the pan and arrange them in the prepared baking dish.

Heat the remaining 2 tablespoons of oil in the same skillet. Add the onions and garlic and sauté until tender. Stir in the parsley, rosemary, thyme, sage, salt, celery seeds, and pepper. Mix well. Stir in the cooked wild rice, cornbread crumbs, and cherries and stir until well combined. Add a little water to moisten if the mixture seems dry.

Preheat the oven to 350°F. Fill each of the mushrooms with a generous amount of stuffing, cover, and bake until heated through, about 15 minutes.

Trim the stems from the chard and discard, keeping the leaves whole. Heat a large saucepan and steam the chard in just the water that clings to the leaves. Drain the chard and sprinkle with the Bragg Liquid Aminos. Arrange the greens on a serving platter, place the mushrooms on top, and serve.

California Nori Rolls Shoshoni-Style

Serves 6 (makes 36 rolls)

Homemade nori rolls are so fresh and delicious. Make them for a light lunch for yourself. Kids love them too! Serve nori rolls as appetizers at a dinner party with Marinated Ginger, page 64. This is a great sattvic or calming recipe that can be enjoyed by everyone.

5 cups water

1 teaspoon salt

3 cups sushi rice or short-grain brown rice

3 tablespoons toasted sesame seeds

3 tablespoons rice vinegar

1 tablespoon honey

1 avocado, sliced thinly

1 carrot, sliced lengthwise in thin strips

1/2 cucumber, peeled, seeded, and sliced lengthwise in thin strips

4 scallions, thinly sliced lengthwise

1/2 cup natural mayonnaise

1 tablespoon natural soy sauce

1 teaspoon prepared wasabi (Japanese horseradish)

6 sheets toasted nori seaweed (sushi nori)

Put the water and salt in a large saucepan and bring to a boil. Add the rice, reduce the heat, cover, and cook until tender, about 20 minutes for sushi rice or 40 to 45 minutes for brown rice. Transfer to a bowl and fluff with a fork.

Combine the sesame seeds, rice vinegar, and honey and pour over the rice. Mix well. Place the rice in the refrigerator to marinate and cool. Prepare the vegetables and arrange on a plate next to your work area. Mix the mayonnaise, soy sauce, and wasabi in a small bowl.

Lay out a bamboo sushi mat and place a nori sheet on top. If you don't have a bamboo mat, lay the nori sheet on a cutting board. Place 1 cup of cooled rice in the center. Wet your hands and press the rice down evenly over the sheet, leaving a 2-inch margin at the top. Spread 1 tablespoon of the mayonnaise mixture over the rice. Lay some of the vegetables (about 1/6 of them, since you will be making 6 rolls) horizontally across the center of the rice.

Starting with the edge closest to you, roll the nori sheet tightly. Moisten the end of the nori sheet with a small amount of water and roll the log back and forth once or twice to seal the edge. Prepare and roll each nori sheet in the same fashion. Wet a very sharp knife and cut each roll into 6 pieces. Arrange on a platter and serve with Marinated Ginger, page 64, and prepared wasabi.

Festival Tacos with Grilled Tempeh

Here is a quick and easy way to make vegetarian tacos.

Heat the oil in a large skillet. Add the cumin seeds and sauté until they turn a shade darker. Add the onion and sauté until translucent. Add the bell pepper and garlic and cook until tender. Stir in the grated tempeh, Bragg Liquid Aminos, and chili powder. Sauté the tempeh until it has browned and absorbed the flavors, about 15 minutes.

Heat the taco shells as directed on the package and stuff them with the seasoned tempeh. Garnish with shredded lettuce, tomatoes, guacamole, and cheese, if desired.

2 tablespoons sunflower oil

2 teaspoons whole cumin seeds

1 onion, minced

1 bell pepper, seeded and finely chopped

2 cloves garlic, minced

1 pound tempeh, grated

2 to 4 tablespoons Bragg Liquid Aminos or natural soy sauce

1 tablespoon chili powder

8 taco shells

Optional garnishes

shredded lettuce

chopped tomatoes

guacamole

grated cheese

Fajitas with Pan-Fried Tempeh

Serves 2 to 3

Fajitas are a fun and delicious way to serve tempeh, and the marinade makes the flavor come alive.

Marinade

1 pound plain tempeh

1/3 cup chopped fresh cilantro

1/4 cup Bragg Liquid Aminos or natural soy sauce

3 tablespoons fresh lime juice

2 tablespoons sunflower oil

2 tablespoons light molasses or honey

1 tablespoon thinly sliced fresh ginger

1 teaspoon minced chipotle chili pepper

1 teaspoon ground coriander

1 clove garlic, minced

1/2 teaspoon ground cumin

Fajitas

3 tablespoons sunflower oil

1 small purple onion, quartered and thinly sliced

1/2 red bell pepper, cut in thin strips

1/2 yellow pepper, cut in thin strips

1/2 cup sliced summer squash (yellow, zucchini, or patty pan)

4 whole wheat tortillas, warmed

in Chipotle Lime Marinade

Drain the tempeh and cut each piece in half lengthwise to make two thin, flat pieces of equal size. Combine the remaining marinade ingredients in a heavy-bottomed skillet. Bring to a boil and add the tempeh. Cover and simmer for 15 minutes. Uncover and continue to cook until the liquid is absorbed, turning the tempeh until it is browned on all sides. Remove from the skillet. Slice into thin strips and set aside.

Heat the remaining 2 tablespoons of sunflower oil in the skillet. Add the onion and sauté until it starts to brown and caramelize. Stir in the peppers and squash and sauté until just tender. Wrap the vegetables and tempeh strips in the warmed tortillas. Serve with side dishes of sour cream and guacamole, if desired.

Grilled BBQ Tofu

Being a Southerner, Shanti missed her family's summer barbeques. She developed this recipe for Shoshoni. It's a favorite for the Fourth of July or for a fun summer picnic served with hot buttered corn on the cob and Vegetarian Caesar Salad, page 41. You also can serve it over brown rice, in pita pockets, or on toasted whole grain buns.

1 pound firm tofu

1 cup sun-dried tomatoes, soaked in hot water to cover for about 10 minutes and drained

1/4 cup Bragg Liquid Aminos or natural soy sauce

1/4 cup rice vinegar

1/4 cup Sucanat or other natural sugar

3 tablespoons toasted sesame oil

3 tablespoons stone-ground mustard

1/4 cup sunflower oil

1 green bell pepper, seeded and thinly sliced

1/4 cup thinly sliced scallions

2 tablespoons toasted sesame seeds

Drain the tofu and press out any extra water by wrapping it in a clean towel and setting a heavy book on top of it for about 10 minutes. Cut the tofu into 4 thin slices lengthwise and set aside.

Combine the soaked and drained sun-dried tomatoes, Bragg Liquid Aminos, rice vinegar, Sucanat, sesame oil, and mustard in a blender and process until smooth. Set aside.

Heat the sunflower oil in a skillet or on a grill and fry the tofu slices until golden brown on both sides. Remove the tofu and add the bell pepper slices to the skillet. Sauté for 5 minutes.

Preheat the oven to 350°F. Pour 1 cup of the blended sauce into the bottom of an 8 x 12-inch glass baking pan and place the tofu on top of the sauce. Pour the remainder of the sauce evenly over the tofu, coating it well. Scatter the green pepper over the tofu and bake uncovered for 30 minutes.

Check the tofu after 15 minutes to make sure it is not getting too dry. If the tofu begins to dry, cover the pan with aluminum foil for the last 15 minutes of baking. Serve garnished with the scallions and toasted sesame seeds.

Tempeh Sloppy Joes with Roasted Red Pepper Sauce

This is another summer favorite served in warm pita pockets, on warm whole grain buns, or as a delicious topping for brown rice.

Heat the sunflower oil in a saucepan. Add the onion and sauté until clear. Add the tempeh and bell peppers and sauté 5 minutes.

2 tablespoons sunflower oil

½ cup chopped onions

1 (8- to 10-ounce) package tempeh, cut in 1-inch cubes

½ cup chopped green bell peppers

2 cups Roasted Red Pepper Sauce, page 109

¼ cup Sucanat or other natural sugar

3 tablespoons Bragg Liquid Aminos or natural soy sauce

2 tablespoons olive oil

1 tablespoon stone-ground mustard

½ teaspoon liquid smoke (optional)

Pepper

¼ cup chopped fresh parsley

Combine the Roasted Red Pepper Sauce, Sucanat, Bragg Liquid Aminos, olive oil, mustard, optional liquid smoke, and pepper in a blender and process until smooth. Pour the sauce into the pan along with the tempeh. Turn down the heat, cover, and simmer for 20 to 30 minutes, stirring often to prevent burning. Add a little water if the mixture gets too dry. Uncover and stir in the parsley.

Vegetable

Side Dishes

Baked Potatoes in Cashew Sauce
with Fresh Chives

These creamy potatoes are steeped in a tasty cashew sauce and topped with fresh garden chives.

Heat the ghee in a skillet. Add the onion and sauté for about 5 minutes or until softened.

2 teaspoons ghee

1/2 onion, minced

6 red potatoes

3 tablespoons barley flour

1/2 cup whole raw cashews

2 cups boiling water

2 teaspoons salt

1/2 teaspoon garlic powder

Generous pinch of pepper

1/4 cup minced fresh chives, minced

Scrub the potatoes well and slice them thinly into rounds. Place the barley flour in a bowl and toss the potato slices in it until they are well coated.

Preheat the oven to 350°F. Lightly oil a deep, glass, 8 x 12-inch baking dish with ghee and arrange the potato slices in the dish. Spoon the onions over the top. Cover with foil and bake for 50 to 60 minutes or until the potatoes are tender when pricked with a fork.

Place the whole cashews in a blender with a 1/2 cup of the boiling water and the salt and garlic powder. Blend until very creamy and smooth. Add the remaining boiling water and pulse a few times to mix. Pour over the potatoes, cover, and bake for 10 minutes. Sprinkle with pepper and garnish with the fresh chives just before serving.

Favorite Grilled Sweet Potatoes

Serves 4

This dish keeps folks coming back for more.

B oil the sweet potatoes until just fork tender. Drain in a colander and set aside to cool.

4 cups peeled and julienned sweet potatoes

2 tablespoons ghee

2 teaspoons whole black mustard seeds

2 tablespoons sesame seeds

2 teaspoons whole cumin seeds

1 teaspoon ground coriander

1/4 cup minced fresh parsley

1/2 teaspoon salt

Pepper

Heat 1 tablespoon of the ghee in a cast-iron skillet. Add the mustard seeds and cover. When the seeds begin to pop, add the sesame seeds and cumin seeds. Continue to cook until they brown. Remove the spices from the pan and set aside.

Heat the remaining ghee in the skillet and fry the sweet potatoes until browned. Add the toasted spices, parsley, salt, and pepper to taste and toss until evenly coated.

Fresh Collards with Toasted Sunflower Seeds
and Vine-Ripened Tomatoes

Greens are good for everyone! The taste and texture of collards is especially appealing. If you have a hard time digesting tomatoes, leave them out and this dish will still be delicious.

Wash the collards thoroughly and slice the leaves from their stems. Discard the stems and chop the leaves into bite-size pieces.

2 bunches of fresh collard greens

2 teaspoons ghee

1/2 onion, quartered and thinly sliced

2 to 4 ripe tomatoes, skinned and chopped

1/2 cup toasted sunflower seeds

2 tablespoons Bragg Liquid Aminos or natural soy sauce

1/4 teaspoon pepper

Heat the ghee in a saucepan or a deep, cast-iron kettle. Add the onions and sauté until browned and caramelized. Add the greens and the tomatoes, cover, and sauté on low heat for 10 minutes. Stir in the sunflower seeds, Bragg Liquid Aminos, and pepper.

Ginger Potato Curry

This curry is just what is needed when you are feeling sluggish. The hot spices really fire up the digestion on cold winter days.

Boil the potatoes uncovered in enough water to cover them for about 20 minutes or until tender. Drain.

2 cups peeled and cubed potatoes

1 tablespoon sunflower oil

1 teaspoon urad dal

½ cup diced red bell peppers

¼ medium onion, chopped fine

1 tablespoon minced fresh ginger

2 teaspoons whole cumin seeds

½ teaspoon dried fenugreek leaves

Heat the sunflower oil in a cast-iron skillet. Add the urad dal and sauté until brown. Stir in the bell peppers, onion, ginger, cumin, and fenugreek leaves and sauté for 3 minutes. Stir in the potatoes and sauté until they are coated with spices and nicely browned.

Green Cabbage Simmered in Curry Spices

Serves 6

Cabbage slowly cooked in warming spices simply melts in your mouth. If you are avoiding dairy, this dish is just as delicious without the yogurt or sour cream.

Heat the ghee in a large skillet. Add the cumin and mustard seeds and fry them over medium heat until the mustard seeds pop. Quickly stir in the onion and garlic. Lower the heat and sauté until the onion is tender, about 5 minutes.

Stir in the tomato, chili, turmeric, and ginger. Cover and let the mixture stew for 5 minutes. Stir in the cabbage, cover, and cook for 30 minutes.

When the cabbage is soft and tender, stir in the Garam Masala and mix well. Stir in the optional yogurt or sour cream, cilantro, cayenne, and salt to taste. Heat gently but do not boil.

2 tablespoons ghee

1 teaspoon whole cumin seeds

1 teaspoon whole black mustard seeds

1/2 onion, finely chopped

1 clove garlic, minced

1 ripe tomato, skinned and diced

2 teaspoons chopped green chili pepper

1 teaspoon turmeric

1/2 teaspoon minced fresh ginger

6 cups finely chopped green cabbage

1 teaspoon Garam Masala, page 70

1/2 cup plain yogurt or low-fat sour cream (optional)

1/4 cup minced fresh cilantro

1/4 teaspoon cayenne

Salt

Golden Baked Curry Potatoes

The curry spice cooks slowly into these oven-roasted potatoes for a wonderfully delicious and simple side dish. Serve it with our Cucumber and Mint Raita, page 60.

Preheat the oven to 350°F. Combine the potatoes, ghee, curry powder, and salt and pepper to taste in a 9 x 13-inch casserole dish. Cover the dish with foil and bake for 20 minutes. Uncover and continue baking 10 to 20 minutes longer or until the potatoes are cooked and nicely browned. Garnish with the cilantro.

6 yellow finn or other tasty potatoes, peeled and sliced in thick julienne

1/4 cup ghee, melted

1 tablespoon curry powder

Salt and pepper

1/4 cup chopped fresh cilantro

Oven-Roasted Green Beans
with Fresh Garden Basil

Serves 6

The addition of fresh garden herbs makes this simple dish shine.

6 cups sliced fresh green beans (cut in 1-inch lengths)

¼ cup ghee, melted

1 tablespoon minced fresh rosemary, or 1 teaspoon dried rosemary

1 tablespoon minced fresh dill, or 1 teaspoon dried dill

1 teaspoon salt

½ cup finely chopped fresh basil

Preheat the oven to 375°F. Place the green beans in a 9 x 13-inch baking dish. Drizzle the beans with the melted ghee, rosemary, and dill. Sprinkle the salt over the top and toss until the beans are evenly coated.

Cover and bake for 20 to 30 minutes, stirring often. Remove the cover and bake 5 to 10 minutes longer or until browned. When the beans are tender, remove from the oven and add the fresh basil and toss until evenly distributed.

Maple-Roasted Parsnips with Caramelized Onion

Parsnips seem largely forgotten in American cuisine. They have a light, sweet flavor and crunchy texture that add interest and variety to everyday foods. We often use parsnips as an alternative to carrots in our Shoshoni cuisine. This dish has deep, rich flavors that are perfect for cold fall and winter days.

2 pounds parsnips, peeled and sliced into ¼-inch-thick rounds

2 tablespoons ghee, melted

2 tablespoons pure maple syrup

¼ teaspoon salt

1 tablespoon ghee

½ onion, thinly sliced

¼ cup finely chopped fresh parsley

Dash of pepper

Preheat the oven to 375°F. Combine the parsnips, melted ghee, maple syrup, and salt in a 9 x 13-inch casserole dish. Bake uncovered for about 30 minutes.

Heat the remaining 1 tablespoon of ghee in a skillet. Add the onion and sauté on low until caramelized, about 15 minutes. Remove the parsnips from the oven, top with the caramelized onion, and sprinkle with the parsley and pepper.

Mixed Greens with Toasted Coconut and Hot Chilies

This dish blends the flavor of hot chilies, sweet coconut, and crunchy almonds with fresh garden greens.

Toast the slivered almonds and coconut in a dry skillet (we prefer to use cast-iron as it distributes the heat evenly) for about 5 minutes or until lightly browned.

3/4 cup blanched slivered almonds

1/2 cup shredded fresh or dried coconut

3 tablespoons ghee or light sesame oil

2 tablespoons natural sugar

1 teaspoon whole black mustard seeds

1 teaspoon whole cumin seeds

2 pounds mixed leafy greens (such as collards, kale, and chard) washed, stemmed, and coarsely chopped

1 tablespoon minced fresh ginger

2 teaspoons seeded and minced hot chilies (optional)

1 teaspoon salt

1/4 teaspoon dried fenugreek leaves

2 tablespoons low-fat sour cream or yogurt (optional)

1/4 teaspoon grated nutmeg

Heat the ghee in a heavy-bottomed saucepan over moderate heat. Add the sugar, mustard seeds, and cumin seeds and fry until the seeds darken and the sugar caramelizes. Stir in the greens, toasted almonds and coconut, ginger, optional chilies, salt, and dried fenugreek leaves. Cover, reduce the heat to low, and cook for 10 minutes. Remove the lid and stir. Add 1/4 cup of water if all the liquid has been absorbed into the dish. It should be just a little saucy. Cook another 5 minutes or until the greens are wilted and tender. Stir in the optional sour cream or yogurt and nutmeg and heat gently for about 2 minutes. Serve immediately.

Pan-Fried Eggplant with Fragrant Masala

This delicious dish cooks in minutes. Serve it as a main course accompanied by Indian basmati rice and Warming Whole Mung Dal with Winter Squash, page 81.

Slice the eggplant in rounds about ¼-inch thick. Toss with the Pitta Spice and set aside for 5 minutes.

1 tablespoon ghee

2 Japanese eggplants (unpeeled)

2 tablespoons Pitta Spice, page 72

Heat the ghee in a cast-iron skillet and add the eggplant. Fry on both sides until golden and soft. Add more ghee as needed if you prefer your eggplant crisp rather than soft.

Potato Tikkis Stuffed with Green Peas

Serves 4 to 6

A favorite at Shoshoni, potato tikkis make an excellent snack or a lovely accent to a delicious Indian meal served with dal, basmati rice, and curried vegetables.

3 large red skin potatoes (about 1 1/4 pounds)

1 teaspoon salt

1/4 teaspoon pepper

1 cup fresh or frozen green peas

2 teaspoons minced fresh ginger

1 teaspoon whole cumin seeds, dry roasted and crushed

1/4 teaspoon Garam Masala, page 70

2 pinches of salt

Olive oil or ghee for pan-frying

Boil the potatoes in their skins until barely tender when pierced by a fork. When they are cool enough to handle, peel and grate by hand or in a food processor fitted with a grating blade. Add 1 teaspoon of salt and 1/4 teaspoon of pepper and mix well. Lightly oil your hands and form the potato mixture into 10 to 12 balls.

Coarsely mash the peas or pulse them for a moment in a food processor fitted with a metal blade to make a coarse meal. Stir in the ginger, crushed cumin seeds, Garam Masala, and salt. Mix well.

With your thumb, make a well in the potato balls and fill with about 1 tablespoon of mashed peas. Gently press to seal the opening and enclose the peas on all sides. Gently flatten the balls into a patty about 1/2-inch thick.

Heat 1 tablespoon of olive oil in a cast-iron skillet or sauté pan and cook the patties over low heat for 5 to 10 minutes on each side or until nicely browned with a thin, crisp crust. Transfer the cooked patties to a paper towel to remove any excess oil. Continue frying the patties until all are cooked, adding more oil to the pan as necessary. Serve hot as is or with any of our chutneys (see pages 53 through 58).

Red Chili Masala Potatoes

This dry curry is delicious served with Sweet Fennel and Tomato Chutney, page 58, and Cucumber Mint Raita, page 60.

Boil the potatoes until just tender, about 10 minutes. Drain.

Heat the ghee in a cast-iron skillet. Add the onion and garlic and sauté until the onion is translucent. Stir in the Pitta Spice, ginger, chili, Garam Masala, cumin, and saffron. Stir to combine. Add the potatoes and fry until crispy and brown. Add a little extra oil if needed to moisten the potatoes.

4 medium russet potatoes, peeled and julienned

1 tablespoon ghee

1/2 small onion, minced

1 clove garlic, minced

2 tablespoons Pitta Spice, page 72

1 teaspoon minced fresh ginger

1 teaspoon minced red chili, or 1/2 teaspoon dried red pepper flakes

1 teaspoon Garam Masala, page 70

1 teaspoon ground cumin

2 pinches saffron threads

Roasted Winter Squash and Bell Peppers

This dish has become a popular staple among the Shoshoni yogis. The delicious flavor of roasted squash, garlic, and peppers is irresistible. We like to serve this dish with Herbed Vegetable Barley Soup, page 90, and Fresh Herb and Baby Greens Salad, page 30.

Preheat the oven to 375°F. Combine all the ingredients in a 9 x 13-inch casserole dish. Mix thoroughly so that the vegetables are well coated with the ghee and herbs.

Bake uncovered for about 30 minutes, stirring occasionally until the squash is tender and the vegetables have browned.

4 cups peeled and cubed butternut squash (1 medium squash)

1 onion, coarsely chopped

1/2 cup thinly sliced red bell peppers

1/2 cup thinly sliced green bell peppers

1/4 cup ghee, melted

1 tablespoon dried herbs (use any combination of rosemary, thyme, dill, and savory)

2 cloves garlic, coarsely chopped

1 teaspoon salt

1/2 teaspoon pepper

Sautéed Cucumbers and Romaine

Toasted sunflower seeds, fresh Romaine lettuce, and garden cucumbers blend beautifully in this unique and elegant side dish.

Slice the cucumbers into 1/4-inch-thick pieces. Heat the oil in a wok or wide skillet and lightly brown the sunflower seeds. Add the cucumbers and sauté for 2 minutes, until they start to look translucent and are barely tender. Stir in the romaine and sauté until it wilts. Remove from the heat and toss with the lemon juice, dill, and salt and pepper to taste.

2 cucumbers peeled, cut in half lengthwise, and seeded

2 tablespoons sesame oil

2 tablespoons raw sunflower seeds

1 head romaine lettuce, sliced in 1-inch strips

Juice of 1 lemon (about 3 tablespoons)

1 tablespoon minced fresh dill, or 1 teaspoon dried dill

Salt and pepper

Sautéed Green Beans and Swiss Chard
with Toasted Urad Dal

This can be served as a curried main dish as part of an Indian meal or a green vegetable side dish.

Heat the ghee in a heavy-bottomed skillet. When the ghee is very hot, add the mustard seeds and cover. Shake the pan (as when making popcorn) until the seeds pop and turn gray. Quickly add the urad dal and sauté until it is browned. Stir in the onion, chili, and ginger, and sauté for 1 minute. Add the green beans and the water, cover, and steam for 10 minutes. Add the chard, cover, and steam 5 minutes longer or until the chard is tender. Season with salt and pepper to taste.

1 teaspoon ghee

1/2 teaspoon whole black mustard seeds

1 teaspoon urad dal

1/4 onion, finely chopped

1/2 fresh green chili, seeded and minced

1 teaspoon minced fresh ginger

2 cups sliced green beans (cut in 1-inch lengths)

1/4 cup water

1 cup finely chopped Swiss chard leaves

1 teaspoon salt

Pinch of pepper

Spicy Masala Green Beans

Cooking for yourself or for two can be delicious and simple. This dish is an appetizing addition to Golden Mung Dal Sambar with Coconut Milk, page 79, for a quick nutritious meal.

Steam the green beans until tender. Heat the ghee in a skillet and fry the onion, chili, ginger, and garlic until golden brown, about 10 minutes. Stir in the cooked green beans and the Rasam Masala and toss until well combined.

2 cups sliced green beans (cut in 1-inch lengths)

1 teaspoon ghee

1/4 onion, finely chopped

1/2 fresh green chili, seeded and minced

1 teaspoon minced fresh ginger

1 clove garlic, minced

Pinch of Rasam Masala, page 72

Spring Asparagus with Luscious Walnut Sauce

Serves 2 to 3

Who can resist the taste of fresh asparagus? When the spring harvest arrives, all the yogis and guests are in heaven. Top simple, steamed asparagus with this luscious walnut sauce for an elegant side dish.

Rinse the asparagus. Snap off and discard the tough ends. Steam the whole stalks until just tender, about 5 minutes.

1 bunch (about ¹/₂ pound) fresh asparagus

¹/₂ cup walnuts

¹/₂ to ³/₄ cup hot water

2 teaspoons fresh lemon juice

¹/₂ teaspoon salt

¹/₄ teaspoon turmeric

Pepper

Place the walnuts, water, lemon juice, salt, turmeric, and pepper to taste in a blender and process until smooth and creamy. Gently warm the sauce over low heat. Serve the steamed asparagus with a ladle of walnut sauce on top.

Steamed Kale with Sliced Dates
and Toasted Pecans

The Shoshoni guests say that this is their favorite recipe for kale. The sweetness of the dates complements the pungent taste of the greens, and the nuts add character and richness.

Rinse the kale and remove and discard the stems. Chop the leaves coarsely and steam them in the water that clings to the leaves until just tender, about 5 to 10 minutes.

2 bunches (about ½ pound) fresh kale

1 leek, finely chopped

1 tablespoon ghee

½ cup toasted pecans, coarsely chopped

¼ cup sliced pitted dates

1 teaspoon ground coriander

½ teaspoon salt

Heat the ghee in a skillet. Add the leeks and sauté until lightly browned, about 5 minutes. Stir in the pecans. Drain the kale and add it to the skillet along with the dates, coriander, and salt. Stir well to blend the spices evenly throughout the greens. Cook and stir until heated through.

Tender Cauliflower in Spiced Cottage Cheese Sauce

Serves 4 to 6

You'll be surprised how delicious and easy cottage cheese sauce can be. It blends particularly well with curry spices. Try as a main dish curry or as a tasty side dish.

Clean the cauliflower and break it into bite-size florets. Place it in a steamer basket and steam until barely tender, about 5 minutes.

1 head of cauliflower

1 tablespoon ghee

2 teaspoons whole cumin seeds

1/2 onion, finely chopped

1/2 teaspoon turmeric

1 cup low-fat cottage cheese

1 tablespoon chickpea flour

1/2 cup fresh or frozen green peas

1/4 cup minced fresh cilantro

1/2 teaspoon salt

Pinch of pepper

Heat the ghee in a saucepan. Add the cumin seeds and sauté until lightly browned. Stir in the onion and turmeric and sauté until the onion is tender, about 5 minutes.

Purée the cottage cheese and chickpea flour in a blender until creamy. Stir into the onion and heat gently. Drain the cauliflower well and add it to the cottage cheese mixture. Stir in the peas, cilantro, salt, and pepper to taste and heat gently until warmed through, about 5 minutes.

Japanese Eggplant and Cauliflower Curry

Young, tender, Japanese eggplant sautéed with fennel, fresh ginger, and coriander is a simple Indian delicacy. Enjoy it as a main dish with Indian basmati rice or as a side dish with Red Chili Masala Potatoes, page 155.

1 tablespoon ghee

1/2 teaspoon whole cumin seeds

1/4 teaspoon whole fennel seeds

1 teaspoon minced fresh ginger

1/2 teaspoon turmeric

1 teaspoon ground coriander

2 medium Japanese eggplants, sliced in rounds about 1/4-inch thick

1/2 medium cauliflower, broken into small florets

1 teaspoon ground cinnamon

Heat the ghee in a cast-iron skillet. Add the cumin and fennel seeds and fry until they are lightly browned. Stir in the ginger and turmeric. Brown them for 1 minute and set aside. Sprinkle the ground coriander over the sliced eggplant and add it to the skillet. Stir in 1/2 cup of water and cook and stir over medium-high heat for about 5 minutes.

Meanwhile, steam the cauliflower in a separate pot until tender. Drain it well and toss it with the cinnamon. Add it to the eggplant and cook and stir for 5 minutes longer or until the flavors are well blended and the eggplant is tender.

Vegetable Pakoras

with Fresh Coconut and Green Chili Chutney

Pakoras are vegetables dipped in a spicy chickpea batter and fried. Use any combination of your favorite vegetables when making these delicious fritters. We indulge in a variety of veggie pakoras for special holiday feasts.

Combine the chickpea flour, ghee, lemon juice, coriander, baking powder, turmeric, cardamom, cumin, cinnamon, cloves, salt to taste, and cayenne. Mix well. Add 5 to 6 tablespoons of the water and beat with an electric mixer until the batter is smooth and free of lumps. Add the remaining water as needed for a smooth batter; it should easily coat a wooden spoon. If the batter is too thick, add a little more water.

Heat the oil in a heavy-bottomed, 3- or 4-quart stainless steel pan. Beat the batter once more to fluff it before using. Dip the vegetables into the batter a few at a time and fry them in the hot oil until browned on all sides and not doughy in the center. Take care not to fry them too quickly. If the oil is too hot, the pakoras will be brown on the outside but raw inside. Drain on paper towels and serve immediately.

Serve with our Fresh Coconut and Green Chili Chutney, page 54.

1¹/₃ cups sifted chickpea flour

2 tablespoons ghee, melted, or vegetable oil

1 tablespoon fresh lemon juice

1 teaspoon ground coriander

¹/₂ teaspoon baking powder

¹/₄ teaspoon turmeric

¹/₄ teaspoon ground cardamom

¹/₄ teaspoon ground cumin

¹/₄ teaspoon ground cinnamon

¹/₄ teaspoon ground cloves

Salt

Pinch of cayenne

9 tablespoons cold water, as needed

2 cups cauliflower florets

2 cups sliced zucchini (cut in 2-inch strips)

1 or 2 large onions, sliced and separated into rings

4 cups vegetable oil for frying

Grains

Fragrant Basmati Rice with Cashews

Most Indian meals are served with basmati rice. The variations are limited only by the imagination. This dish features fragrant cinnamon and cashews.

Heat the butter in a skillet. Add the cashews and sauté until lightly browned, about 5 minutes. Set aside.

2 tablespoons butter

2 tablespoons cashews (whole or halves)

1 1/2 cups white basmati rice

3 cups water

1/2 stick cinnamon

1/2 teaspoon salt

Pinch of pepper

1/2 cup fresh or frozen green peas (optional)

Rinse the basmati rice twice using a strainer. Bring the water to a boil in a heavy-bottomed pot with tight-fitting lid. Add the cinnamon, salt, and pepper. Add the rice, stir, and bring to a boil. Cover and turn the heat to low. Cook for 20 minutes or until all the water is absorbed. Stir in the optional peas, cover, and let rest 5 minutes for the peas to become tender and warm. Stir in the browned cashews and serve.

Bulgur Pilaf

Bulgur is cracked wheat and is most commonly used in Middle Eastern cooking. Serve this simple dish with Mediterranean Red Lentil and Spinach Stew with Currants, page 91, and Fresh Herb and Baby Greens Salad, page 30, topped with Moroccan Vinaigrette, page 50. Faith's Armenian friend, Annahid Katchian, taught her this sumptuous dish.

Heat the olive oil in a saucepan. Add the dry vermicelli and fry until browned. Add the vegetable stock and bring to a boil. Simmer 5 minutes or until the vermicelli is almost tender. Add the bulgur and cook 5 minutes over low heat until it is tender. Remove from the heat, cover, and let stand for 10 minutes.

¼ cup olive oil

3 ounces vermicelli, broken into 2-inch pieces

6 cups vegetable stock or water

3 cups fine bulgur

2 tablespoons ghee or light sesame oil

1 onion, thinly sliced

¼ cup minced fresh parsley

Heat the ghee in a skillet. Add the onion and sauté 5 to 10 minutes or until tender. Stir the onion and fresh parsley into the pilaf and serve.

Creole Red Bean Jambalaya

Serves 4 to 6

Here is another of Shanti's Louisiana favorites! This jambalaya is full of flavor and can be served as a main dish accompanied by Fresh Collards with Toasted Sunflower Seeds and Vine-Ripe Tomatoes, page 146.

2 teaspoons ghee

¼ cup minced onion

2 cloves garlic, minced

¼ cup chopped celery

¼ cup diced red bell pepper

¼ cup diced green bell pepper

2 teaspoons paprika

½ green chili, seeded and minced

1 teaspoon chili powder

1 teaspoon ground cumin

½ teaspoon dried thyme

½ teaspoon dried sage

2½ cups vegetable broth or water

2 cups cooked and drained red chili beans or kidney beans

1 cup white basmati rice

¼ cup Bragg Liquid Aminos or natural soy sauce

2 teaspoon salt

¼ cup minced fresh parsley

Generous pinch of pepper

Heat the ghee in a saucepan. Add the onion and garlic and sauté until tender, about 5 minutes. Stir in the chopped celery, bell peppers, paprika, green chili, chili powder, cumin, thyme, and sage and sauté for 5 minutes. Add the vegetable broth, beans, rice, Bragg Liquid Aminos, and salt and bring to a boil. Cover and simmer on low for 15 minutes.

When the rice is tender, add the fresh parsley and pepper and fluff gently with a fork.

Curried Barley and Swiss Chard

Barley is an ancient grain not widely used in our culture today. In Ayurvedic diets it is beneficial in the springtime for cleansing the body.

2/3 cup pearl barley

1 teaspoon ghee

1 teaspoon whole cumin seeds

2 bay leaves

1/2 teaspoon turmeric

4 cups water

1 teaspoon salt

1 cup finely chopped Swiss chard

Rinse and drain the barley. Heat the ghee in a saucepan. Add the cumin seeds and sauté until lightly browned. Stir in the barley, bay leaves, and turmeric and sauté for 1 minute. Add the water and salt and bring to a boil. Cover, reduce the heat to low, and simmer for 45 to 50 minutes. Stir in the chard, cover, and cook 10 minutes longer or until the barley is tender.

Fennel, Raisin, and Walnut Rice

This is a simple way to jazz up your brown rice. The flavors of fennel, raisins, and toasted walnuts blend very well.

1 cup brown basmati rice

1 tablespoon ghee

1 teaspoon whole fennel seeds

2 cups boiling water

½ cup shredded carrots

¼ cup raisins

½ teaspoon salt

¼ cup walnuts

¼ cup minced fresh parsley

Rinse and drain the rice. Heat the ghee in a heavy-bottomed pot. Add the fennel seeds and toast until lightly browned. Add the rice, water, carrots, raisins, and salt. Bring to a boil, and turn down to simmer, cover and cook for 30 to 40 minutes.

Toast the walnuts in a dry skillet until golden brown. Alternatively, toast them in a 350°F oven on a baking sheet or in a roasting pan for about 10 minutes. When cool, chop them coarsely. When the rice is fully cooked, fluff with a fork. Gently stir in the walnuts and garnish with the parsley just before serving.

Indian Fried Rice

with Pistachios, Fresh Spinach, and Tofu

Serves 4

This special holiday pilaf brings exclamations of delight from our guests. The sweet flavors of fresh tomatoes, pistachios, and fragrant spices team up with pan-fried tofu to make a nutritious side dish.

Rinse the rice in a strainer. Drain.

1 cup white basmati rice

4 tablespoons ghee or sesame oil

2 cups cubed firm tofu

2 tablespoons natural sugar

1 1/2 teaspoons whole cumin seeds

1 teaspoon whole black mustard seeds

2 ripe tomatoes, diced

2 teaspoons ground coriander

3/4 teaspoon turmeric

1/4 teaspoon grated nutmeg

1/4 teaspoon cayenne

1 3/4 to 2 cups water

1 teaspoon salt

8 ounces fresh spinach, washed, stemmed, and coarsely chopped

1/3 cup shelled pistachios

1 1/4 teaspoons fresh lemon juice

Heat 3 tablespoons of the ghee in a saucepan. Add the tofu and fry until it is browned all over. Remove from the pan and drain on paper towels.

Add the sugar, cumin seeds, and black mustard seeds to the skillet. Sauté until the sweetener caramelizes and turns a rich brown color. Add the tomatoes and immediately follow with the coriander, turmeric, nutmeg, cayenne, and rice. Stir-fry for 1 minute; then add the water and salt. Bring to a full boil, lower the heat, cover, and cook for 20 to 25 minutes.

When the rice is fully cooked, fluff with a fork. Heat the remaining 1 tablespoon of ghee in a large skillet. Add the spinach and sauté until tender and bright green, about 3 to 5 minutes. Quickly add the rice, fried tofu, and pistachios. Gently stir-fry for about 3 minutes. Season with the fresh lemon juice and serve.

Kasha with Brown Rice and Caramelized Onions

Serves 6

Toasting the kasha gives it a nutty flavor. This is the perfect dish to make with leftover brown rice or you can prepare both grains fresh. The sweetness of the caramelized onions adds a lot of character to this dish.

1 cup toasted kasha

1 egg white (optional)

2 1/2 cups boiling water

1/2 cup diced carrots

1/2 teaspoon salt

1 tablespoon ghee

1 small onion, thinly sliced

2 cups cooked short-grain brown rice (about 1 cup dry)

1/4 cup thinly sliced scallions

Pepper (optional)

Place the kasha in a saucepan. Whisk in the optional egg white and stir to distribute it evenly. Toast over medium heat, stirring constantly for 1 minute.

Add the water, carrots, and salt and bring to a boil. Lower the heat, cover, and cook for 10 minutes.

Meanwhile, heat the ghee in a large skillet. Add the onions and sauté them until golden brown, about 10 minutes. Add the cooked brown rice, cooked kasha, and scallions to the skillet and stir-fry for 5 to 10 minutes. Season with a dash of pepper, if desired.

Stir-Fried Rice with Whole Cashews

Serves 4 to 6 as a main dish

The rich flavor of roasted cashews added to this simple vegetable fried rice makes an extra special treat.

Rinse and drain the rice. Place it in a large pot along with the water, 1 tablespoon of the sesame oil, and the salt. Bring to a boil, reduce the heat, cover, and simmer for 30 to 40 minutes.

Meanwhile heat the remaining 2 tablespoons of oil in a skillet. Add the onions, ginger, and garlic and sauté until lightly browned. Stir in the mushrooms and sauté until tender. Add the carrots and sauté until tender. Stir in the peppers and cashews and sauté briefly, about 5 minutes.

When the rice is tender, add it to the skillet along with the sprouts, Bragg Liquid Aminos, and scallions. Toss to mix well and serve.

2 cups short-grain brown rice

4 cups boiling water

3 tablespoons toasted sesame oil

1 teaspoon salt

1/2 cup minced onions

2 tablespoons minced fresh ginger

2 cloves garlic, minced

1 cup stemmed and sliced fresh shiitake mushrooms

1/2 cup diced carrots

1/2 cup diced green or red bell peppers

1/4 cup raw whole cashews

1/2 cup mung bean sprouts

1/4 cup Bragg Liquid Aminos or natural soy sauce

1/4 cup thinly sliced scallions

Southwestern-Style Quinoa Pilaf

Some people are a little timid about trying new grains, but quinoa is one of the most nutritious grains available. It blends beautifully with sweet corn and toasted cumin seeds.

1 tablespoon sunflower oil

2 teaspoons whole cumin seeds

1/2 onion, finely chopped

1 1/2 cups water

1 cup quinoa, rinsed and drained

1 cup cooked or canned Anasazi, pinto, or black beans (optional)

1/2 cup sliced yellow summer squash or zucchini

1/2 cup fresh or frozen corn kernels

1/4 cup chopped red bell peppers

2 teaspoons salt

1/4 cup chopped fresh cilantro

2 tablespoons fresh lime or lemon juice

1/4 teaspoon pepper

Heat the oil in a large saucepan. Add the cumin seeds and brown them for 1 minute. Add the onion and sauté until tender, about 10 minutes. Stir in the water, quinoa, optional beans, squash, corn, bell peppers, and salt. Cover tightly and simmer about 10 minutes or until the quinoa is done.

Remove from the heat and let sit covered for 5 minutes. Add the cilantro, lime juice, and pepper, and fluff with a fork.

Toasted Almond and Chili Pepper Rice

This is a simple way to add flavor and color to an Indian feast. Serve with any curry or dal.

Dry-roast the cumin and fennel seeds in a saucepan for about 5 minutes or until the cumin is aromatic. Stir in the water, rice, carrots, ghee, salt, coriander, chili powder, and chili. Bring to a boil, cover, and simmer on low heat for about 15 minutes or until the rice is tender. Gently fluff with a fork. Add the almonds just before serving.

1 teaspoon whole cumin seeds

1/4 teaspoon whole fennel seeds

2 cups water

1 cup white basmati rice

1 cup shredded carrots

1 tablespoon ghee

2 teaspoons salt

1 teaspoon ground coriander

1/2 teaspoon chili powder

1/2 small red chili pepper, seeded and minced

1/4 cup (about 1 ounce) toasted almonds, coarsely chopped

Khicharis

Khichari is a stew typically made of mung beans and rice. It is most often used during an Ayurvedic cleanse to nourish but not overtax the digestion. However, khichari can be a delicious and easy meal any time you like. We have come up with many variations using every kind of vegetable and spice. Don't be afraid to be creative!

Time Saver Method

The dal and rice can be cooked together in a pressure cooker to save time. Follow the manufacturer's directions for filling the pressure cooker. Never fill a pressure cooker more than half full. Use an equal or greater amount of water to beans and rice. For example, for 2 cups total of raw rice and dal use 2 to 3 cups of vegetable stock or water. The water should cover the beans and rice. Bring up to pressure, reduce the heat just enough to maintain full pressure, and cook for 15 minutes. Run the pressure cooker under cold water to cool or follow the manufacturer's directions for quick-releasing the pressure. Do not remove the lid until all the pressure has been released.

Sauté or steam the vegetables in a separate pan or skillet. Add the cooked vegetables and spices to the dal and cook over low heat for about 5 to 10 minutes to blend the flavors. Adjust the seasonings if necessary and serve.

Cooling Sattvic Khichari

Sattwa is the balancing quality or energy of a food that promotes meditation and a tranquil mind.

Rinse the rice and dal in a strainer. Drain and set aside. Heat the ghee in a saucepan. Add the cumin seeds and toast them for 1 minute, taking care that they do not burn. Add the rice, dal, and vegetable stock. Bring to a boil, reduce the heat, cover, and cook until the dal is tender, about 45 minutes. Stir in the carrot, zucchini, and saffron threads. Cover and cook 10 minutes or until the vegetables are tender. Season with salt to taste. Stir in the cilantro or serve it on the side as a garnish. Serve hot.

½ cup white basmati rice

¼ cup green or golden mung dal

1 tablespoon ghee

2 teaspoons whole cumin seeds

4 cups vegetable stock or water

1 small carrot, diced

1 small zucchini, diced

Pinch of saffron threads

1 teaspoon salt

¼ cup chopped fresh cilantro

Barley Vegetable Khichari with Burdock Root

Serves 4 to 6

Barley is a welcome change for Kapha types when springtime arrives. The addition of burdock root is cleansing to the blood.

Rinse the barley and dal. Drain well and set aside. Heat the ghee in a large saucepan. Add the mustard seeds and fry until they pop and turn gray. Quickly stir in the cumin seeds, coriander seeds, turmeric, and ginger. Sauté for just a few seconds, then stir in the water, green beans, Swiss chard, carrot, optional burdock root, and bay leaf. Bring to a boil, cover, and simmer on low for 45 to 50 minutes or until the barley and dal are soft. Stir in the salt and ground coriander.

1/2 cup pearl barley

1/3 cup golden mung dal

1 tablespoon ghee

1 teaspoon whole mustard seeds

1 teaspoon whole cumin seeds

1/2 teaspoon whole coriander seeds

1 teaspoon turmeric

1 teaspoon minced fresh ginger

6 cups water

1 cup sliced green beans (cut in 1-inch lengths)

1 cup finely chopped Swiss chard

1 carrot, peeled and diced

3 inches burdock root, cut in 1-inch pieces (optional)

1 bay leaf

2 teaspoons salt

1 teaspoon ground coriander

Mountain Yogi Khichari

The mountain yogis at Shoshoni need a hearty warming khichari for winter evenings by the fire. This dish can be a meal by itself, providing protein, vegetables, and warming spices to fire up the digestion.

Rinse the dal and rice and drain. Heat the ghee in a saucepan. Add the cumin seeds and lightly toast them for about 1 minute. Stir in the onions, ginger, and chili and sauté until tender. Add the water, dal, rice, green beans, sweet potatoes, collard greens, turmeric, cinnamon stick, and cardamom. Cover and cook on low to medium heat for 30 minutes.

When the rice and dal are fully cooked, remove the cinnamon stick and stir in the cilantro, salt, and coriander.

¼ cup golden mung dal

¼ cup white basmati rice

1 tablespoon ghee

½ teaspoon whole cumin seeds

½ cup minced onions

1 teaspoon minced fresh ginger

½ green chili, seeded and minced

4 cups water

½ cup sliced green beans (in 2-inch lengths)

½ cup peeled and cubed sweet potatoes

½ cup finely chopped collard greens

1 teaspoon turmeric

1 cinnamon stick

½ teaspoon ground cardamom

3 tablespoons minced fresh cilantro

1 teaspoon salt

1 teaspoon ground coriander

 Spicy Springtime Khichari

Serves 4 to 6

Khichari is such a satisfying and nourishing meal anytime. This one has a little extra pep for a weak digestive fire.

¼ cup green or golden mung dal

¼ cup white basmati rice

1 teaspoon ghee

½ teaspoon whole mustard seeds

½ teaspoon whole cumin seeds

¼ teaspoon whole fenugreek seeds

¼ teaspoon whole fennel seeds

¼ teaspoon whole coriander seeds

½ teaspoon turmeric

1 bay leaf

4 cups vegetable stock or water

1 carrot, finely chopped

1 cup finely chopped green beans

½ inch fresh ginger, minced

½ green chili, seeded and minced

¼ cup minced fresh cilantro

2 teaspoons salt

1 teaspoon ground coriander

Rinse the dal and rice and drain well. Heat the ghee in a saucepan until very hot. Quickly stir in the mustard seeds and cover until they pop and turn gray. Add the cumin seeds, fenugreek seeds, fennel seeds, coriander seeds, turmeric, and bay leaf, and brown them for 1 minute. Stir in the water, carrot, green beans, ginger, and chili. Bring to a boil, cover, reduce the heat, and simmer for 30 minutes or until the dal is soft. Stir in the cilantro, salt, and coriander.

Warming Winter Khichari

The warming spices in this khichari will sustain you through the coldest winter months.

Rinse the rice and dal and drain well. Heat the ghee in a saucepan until very hot. Add the mustard seeds and cook until they pop and turn gray. Quickly stir in the onions, cumin seeds, turmeric, ginger, chili, and asafetida. Sauté until lightly browned. Add the water, rice, dal, green beans, potatoes, and carrot. Bring to a boil, cover, reduce the heat, and simmer for 30 minutes. Stir in the cilantro and salt.

½ cup white basmati rice

¼ cup green or golden mung dal

1 teaspoon ghee

1 teaspoon whole mustard seeds

½ cup minced onions

1 teaspoon whole cumin seeds

½ teaspoon turmeric

½ inch fresh ginger, minced

½ hot green chili, seeded and minced

Pinch of asafetida

4 cups water

1 cup sliced green beans (in 2-inch lengths)

1 cup peeled and cubed potatoes or sweet potatoes

1 small carrot, diced

¼ cup chopped fresh cilantro

1½ teaspoons salt

Yeasted, Quick, and Savory-Filled Breads

Coconut Curry Calzones

Serves 4 as a dinner of rice and curry and
6 calzones, or makes 12 calzones

*You can enjoy the Coconut Milk Vegetable Curry on its own, too. It makes
a wonderful meal served with basmati rice and dal.*

Coconut Milk Vegetable Curry

5 medium potatoes, peeled and
diced (about 4 cups)

2 cups peeled and diced winter
squash (acorn squash, butternut,
or pumpkin)

1 cup sliced fresh green beans (cut
in 1-inch lengths)

2 tablespoons ghee or olive oil

1 onion, finely chopped

1 red or green bell pepper, seeded
and coarsely chopped

2 tablespoons Madras curry
powder, homemade (see page 74)
or store-bought

1 inch fresh ginger, peeled and
minced (about 2 tablespoons)

1 (14-ounce) can coconut milk

1 cup fresh straw mushrooms,
wiped clean, or 1 (15-ounce) can
straw mushrooms, drained

1 cup cashews, browned in 2
tablespoons ghee or olive oil

2 tablespoons minced fresh basil,
or 2 teaspoons dried basil

Salt

Pepper

Cayenne

1 or 2 bananas (Hawaiian apple
bananas, if available)

Two meals in one! This coconut milk curry is delicious served with basmati rice and your favorite dal. We make enough of the curry so that there are leftovers. Faith created this dish fusing Thai-style curry with Italian-style calzones. She explains, "One day while making homemade bread, I remembered that I had some leftover coconut milk curry in the fridge. I got the idea of wrapping the curry inside my bread dough and making something like curried calzones. They were so delicious! We found they tasted great warm or cold, and I began making them to take with us whenever we travel."

Place the potatoes, winter squash, and green beans in a 3-quart saucepan with 4 cups water. Bring to a boil, reduce the heat, cover, and steam for about 30 minutes or until tender. Remove from the heat and drain off the water.

Heat the ghee in a skillet. Add the onion and bell pepper and sauté for 5 minutes or until softened. Stir in the curry powder and ginger and sauté for 5 minutes. (Sautéing the curry powder gives it a richer flavor.) Stir in half of the coconut milk and remove from the heat. Stir the sautéed mixture into the pot of steamed vegetables. Add the remaining coconut milk, straw mushrooms, browned cashews, and basil. Season with salt, pepper, and cayenne to taste. Garnish with the sliced banana.

Red Onion Bread (for calzones)

Makes enough for 12 curried calzones,
or 6 calzones and 1 loaf of bread

Combine the whole wheat flour, onion, sugar, yeast, and salt in a large bowl. Mix well.

3¹/₂ cups whole wheat flour

¹/₂ cup minced red onion

¹/₃ cup natural sugar

2 packages (2 tablespoons) active dry yeast

2 teaspoons salt

2 cups water

2¹/₂ to 3 cups unbleached white flour

¹/₃ cup olive oil

2 eggs

1 egg beaten with 2 tablespoons water (for egg wash for top of calzones)

Heat the water in a saucepan until very warm (about 120°F to 130°F). Stir in the oil and add to the flour mixture. Add the 2 eggs and mix by hand until moistened. Alternatively, use an electric mixer with a dough hook and mix for 3 minutes on medium speed. Gradually stir in enough of the unbleached white flour to make a firm dough. Knead the dough on a lightly floured surface for 5 to 8 minutes.

Place the dough in an oiled bowl, turning to coat with a light layer of oil. Cover and let rise in a warm place for about 30 minutes or until doubled in size.

Preheat the oven to 350°F. Lightly oil one or two baking sheets (you'll need one sheet for 6 calzones or two sheets for 12 calzones).

Punch down the dough and divide in half. Further divide one half into 6 small balls. Use a rolling pin to roll the small balls into circles, about 6 inches in diameter. (The dough should be fairly thin.) Place about $1/2$ cup of the coconut curry in the center and top with 2 or 3 slices of banana. Moisten the edge of the dough with water and fold the dough over the filling, pressing the edges together to form a half-moon shape.

Place the stuffed calzone on the prepared baking sheet and continue. When you have filled the baking sheet, brush the tops of the calzones with the egg wash and bake for about 25 minutes or until browned and puffed.

Form the remaining dough into 6 additional calzones and stuff as directed. Alternatively, shape the remaining dough into a loaf of bread (either a round loaf on a baking sheet or place in a bread pan) and bake for 35 to 40 minutes until browned and baked through.

Sumptuous Artichoke Calzones

Try these delicious pastries as a special dinner treat with a ladle of Savory Red Sauce, page 109, over the top.

Dough

1½ cups warm water

1 package (1 tablespoon) active
   dry yeast

3 cups whole wheat flour

½ cup unbleached white flour

2 tablespoons olive oil

1½ teaspoons salt

1 tablespoon natural sugar

Place the warm water in a large bowl. Add the yeast and stir until it is dissolved. Stir in the remaining ingredients and mix well. Turn the dough onto a floured surface and knead for 10 minutes. Transfer the dough to a lightly oiled bowl and turn once. Cover with a damp towel and let rise in a warm place for 1 hour.

with Eggplant and Cottage Cheese

Filling

6 tablespoons sunflower
   or olive oil

$1/2$ small onion, minced

2 cloves garlic, minced

1 cup chopped artichoke hearts

6 cups peeled and diced eggplant

$1/2$ cup roasted red pepper slices

$1 1/2$ cups cottage cheese

$1/2$ cup chopped fresh basil leaves

Salt

Heat 2 tablespoons of the oil in a saucepan. Add the onion and garlic and sauté until browned. Add the artichoke hearts and sauté 2 to 3 minutes. Transfer to a large bowl and stir in the red pepper slices. In the same saucepan, add the remaining oil and sauté the eggplant until tender. Add to the bowl with the onion and artichoke hearts. In a separate small bowl, combine the cottage cheese and basil and season with a pinch of salt to taste.

To assemble

Preheat the oven to 375°F. Lightly oil a baking sheet.

Divide the dough into 6 balls. Roll out one ball at a time into a circle about $1/8$-inch thick and 6 or 7 inches in diameter. Place $1/2$ cup of the vegetable filling in the center along with $1/4$ cup of the cottage cheese. Fold the dough over the filling and seal the edges all the way around with the back of a fork. Brush with a little olive oil and place on the prepared baking sheet. Bake the calzones for 30 to 35 minutes or until golden brown. Top with a ladle of Savory Red Sauce, page 109, if desired.

Fresh Italian Herb and Roasted Garlic Focaccia

Serves 6 (makes 6 large squares or 12 smaller squares)

1 head of garlic

Olive oil

1^1/2 cups warm water

2 tablespoons natural sugar

1 package (1 tablespoon) active
dry yeast

2 tablespoons olive oil

1^1/2 teaspoons salt

3 to 3^1/2 cups unbleached white
flour

^{1}/2 to 1 cup whole wheat flour

^{1}/2 cup olive oil

^{1}/4 cup minced fresh basil, or
2 tablespoons dried basil

^{1}/4 cup minced fresh rosemary, or
2 tablespoons dried rosemary

^{1}/2 teaspoon coarsely ground
pepper

Freshly grated Parmesan or
Romano cheese (optional)

Preheat the oven to 400°F. Place the whole head of garlic in a baking dish. Drizzle a little olive oil over it and bake for 30 minutes. Remove from the oven and let cool.

Meanwhile, combine the water, sugar, and yeast in a bowl and stir until the yeast is dissolved. Stir in the 2 tablespoons olive oil and salt. Add the flours and mix well until the dough forms a ball. Transfer to a floured surface and knead for 10 minutes. Lightly oil a large bowl with olive oil. Place the dough in the bowl and turn it once to coat it with oil. Cover with a clean, damp towel and leave it in a warm place to rise for 45 to 60 minutes or until doubled in size.

Preheat the oven to 400°F. Punch down the dough and transfer it onto a floured surface. With a rolling pin, roll the dough into a 10 x 12-inch rectangle about ^{1}/2-inch thick. Place the rectangle in a lightly oiled 16 x 11-inch jelly roll pan and press it into the edges of the pan as evenly as you can. Press your fingertips into the dough many times making little holes all over the surface. Drizzle ^{1}/2 cup of olive oil over the top and let rise again in a warm place for about 15 minutes or until the dough has risen evenly.

Flavorful focaccia is an elegant, delicious accompaniment to Spinach Fettuccine with Almond Basil Sauce, page 118, or Fresh Spinach and Basil Pesto Stuffed Shells with Savory Red Sauce, page 108.

Bake the bread for 30 minutes or until golden brown.

To prepare the roasted garlic, squeeze the garlic cloves into a small bowl and mash into a paste. Using a pastry brush or rubber spatula, brush the garlic paste evenly and equally over the top of the baked bread. Sprinkle with the herbs, pepper, and optional cheese, if desired. Serve the bread with a dish of your best olive oil on the side for dipping.

Yeasted, Quick, and Savory-Filled Breads

Greek-Style Pizza with Garden Tomatoes and Tofu Feta

Homemade pizza is such a treat! This version serves up an oven-fresh crust topped simply with virgin olive oil, fresh tomatoes, Italian basil, and our special recipe of Tofu Feta, page 67. Dairy lovers can substitute real feta cheese, if they prefer.

Combine the warm water, sugar, and yeast in a large bowl, stirring well to dissolve the yeast. Stir in the olive oil and salt. Add the flours and stir until a ball of dough is formed.

Transfer the dough to a floured surface and knead for 10 minutes. Oil the bowl with a little olive oil. Put the dough into the bowl and turn it so it is coated with the oil. Cover with a clean towel and put it in a warm spot to rise. Let the dough rise for 30 minutes or until doubled in size.

Preheat the oven to 375°F. Punch down the dough and turn it out onto the counter again. Divide in half and form into two balls of equal size. Roll out each ball thinly or thickly, depending on your preference, and fit them into a 12-inch pizza pan. Brush the crusts with a little more olive oil and set aside to rest for 10 minutes. Top the crusts equally with the tomatoes, Tofu Feta, and fresh basil, and drizzle with a little olive oil. Bake for 20 minutes or until the crust is golden brown.

Pizza crust

1½ cups warm water

2 tablespoons Sucanat or other natural sugar

1 package (1 tablespoon) active dry yeast

2 tablespoons extra-virgin olive oil

1½ teaspoons salt

3 to 3½ cups unbleached white flour

½ to 1 cup whole wheat flour

Topping

2 cups thinly sliced, ripe Roma tomatoes

2 cups Tofu Feta, page 67

½ cup minced fresh basil

Extra-virgin olive oil

Sweet Potato Biscuits

Makes 15 to 20 biscuits

Plan ahead to make these delicious biscuits. Serve baked sweet potatoes the night before and put an extra one in the oven to save preparation and cooking time.

Preheat the oven to 375°F. Lightly oil a baking sheet.

Combine the flour, baking powder, salt, and baking soda in a large bowl. Mix well. Cut in the butter with a pastry blender or two forks until well combined.

2 cups whole wheat pastry flour

1 tablespoon baking powder

1 teaspoon salt

1/4 teaspoon baking soda

1/4 cup unsalted butter

1 cooked sweet potato, or about 3/4 cup mashed sweet potato

1/4 cup milk or plain soymilk

3 tablespoons fresh lemon juice

Combine the mashed sweet potato, milk, and lemon juice, beating well with a wire whisk. Pour into the flour mixture, mix well, and form into a ball of dough. Knead gently, just to combine, but avoid over-kneading.

Roll out the dough on a very lightly floured surface until it is about 1 inch thick. Using a biscuit cutter or a small drinking glass, cut the biscuits and place on the prepared baking sheet. If you prefer big, fluffy, soft biscuits, place them on the sheet so that they are touching. If you prefer flaky biscuits that are crispy on the outside, place them about one inch apart. Bake for about 20 minutes or until golden brown.

Old-Style Potato Pierogis

Serves 6 (makes about 24 pierogis)

This recipe comes to us from Narayani, one of our young Shoshoni cooks. We teach our new yogis what we know about cooking and learn some new things from them too! Narayani's dad taught her some dishes from her ethnic heritage. Pierogis are an Eastern European or Polish dish, something like a potato-filled ravioli. We dish up about four pierogis per person as an entrée. They are great served along side a bowl of hot borscht (beet soup) topped with a dollop of sour cream or yogurt.

Have ready

3 cups mashed potatoes (see note below)

Dough

3 cups unbleached white flour

1 cup mashed potatoes

1/2 cup water

1/4 cup canola or olive oil

2 teaspoons salt

Filling

2 cups mashed potatoes

1/2 cup cottage cheese

1/2 small onion, minced (about 1/4 cup)

2 tablespoons ghee or butter

1 1/2 teaspoons salt

1/4 teaspoon pepper

Topping

2 tablespoons canola or olive oil

1 large red or white onion, sliced
   into thin rings (about 1 1/2 cups)

1 cup thinly sliced button,
   chanterelle or shiitake
   mushrooms (about 2 ounces)

For pan-frying

1/4 cup of canola or olive oil

Note: If you do not have leftover mashed potatoes on hand, you can prepare them fresh. Peel and dice 3 medium potatoes; this will equal about 3 cups. Boil the potatoes in water to cover (about 4 cups water) for about 25 minutes or until tender. Drain and mash well. Beat with a wire whisk until smooth.

To prepare the dough, combine the flour, 1 cup mashed potatoes, water, 1/4 cup canola oil, and 2 teaspoons salt in a large bowl. Mix well. Knead the dough until smooth and slightly elastic, about 5 minutes on a lightly floured surface, or about 3 minutes using an electric mixer fitted with a dough hook. The dough should look and feel similar to pasta dough. Lightly oil a clean bowl. Place the dough in the bowl, cover with a cloth, and let rest for 30 minutes. (The dough will not rise but resting will make it easier to roll out.)

While the dough is resting, prepare the filling. Combine the 2 cups mashed potatoes, cottage cheese, minced onion, ghee, salt, and pepper in a large bowl. Mix well.

Fill a large, wide soup pot or saucepan with about 6 inches of water and bring to a boil in preparation for boiling the pierogis.

To prepare the topping, heat the 2 tablespoons canola oil in a skillet. Add the sliced onion and mushrooms and sauté until tender, about 5 minutes. Set aside.

To assemble, roll out about 1 cup of the dough at a time on a lightly floured surface. Roll the dough very thin, about ⅛-inch thick. Cut 3-inch circles with a pastry cutter to make half-moon-shaped pierogis, or cut them in 2 x 4-inch rectangles for square-shaped pierogis. Place about 1 tablespoon of filling in the center of each circle or rectangle. Fold in half and pinch to seal shut. (Note: The dough sticks together well, provided it has not picked up too much flour during rolling. If the edges of your pierogis don't seem to be sticking together well, spread a very thin band of water along the edge with your fingertip and then pinch to seal.)

Drop the pierogis 5 or 6 at a time into the boiling water. Cook them for about 5 minutes at a gentle, rolling boil until they are tender and float. They should look like cooked pasta or raviolis. Check one to be sure they are done. The dough should be tender and cooked through. Remove with a slotted spoon and transfer to a lightly oiled 9 x 12-inch glass baking dish. Continue cooking in this fashion until all the dumplings are boiled and transferred to the baking dish.

Brush a large skillet or sauté pan with a little of the canola oil (about 1 tablespoon) and pan-fry the pierogis over medium heat until golden brown on both sides, about 3 minutes per side. Transfer to a serving dish and continue pan-frying until all the pierogis are browned, adding more oil to the skillet as necessary. Garnish each serving with a portion of the mushroom topping.

Whole Grain Challah

This is a rich, beautiful bread for special occasions.

Sponge

¼ cup warm water

3 tablespoons Sucanat or other
  natural sugar

2 packages (2 tablespoons) active
  dry yeast

Dough

2 cups warm water

3 eggs, lightly beaten

¼ cup canola oil

1 tablespoon salt

4 cups unbleached white flour

2½ to 3 cups whole wheat flour

Egg Wash

1 egg, beaten

1 to 2 tablespoons poppy seeds or
  sesame seeds

To make the sponge, whisk the ¼ cup warm water, sugar, and yeast in a large bowl until frothy. Cover and set aside in a warm place for 10 minutes.

To make the dough, add 2 cups warm water, 3 beaten eggs, oil, salt, unbleached white flour, and 2 cups of the whole wheat flour to the sponge. Mix well to form a ball of dough. Turn the dough out onto a floured surface and knead for 7 to 10 minutes. Oil a large bowl with canola oil to lightly cover the surface. This keeps the dough from sticking to the bowl as it rises. Place the dough in the oiled bowl, turn to coat, cover with a damp towel, and let rise for about 30 minutes or until doubled in size. Punch down and let rise again until it becomes a little airy, about 15 minutes. Punch down, divide in half, and roll into 2 balls.

Punch down each ball of dough. Starting with one ball of dough, divide it into 3 pieces. Roll each piece into a long rope. Pinch all three ropes together at the top and begin to braid. (Bring the outer rope on the right side over the middle rope then bring the left outer rope over the middle one, etc.) When you have finished the braid, tuck the ends under and place on an oiled baking sheet. Repeat with the other ball of dough.

Preheat the oven to 375°F. Brush the tops of the braids with a little more oil and let rise covered with a dry cloth or clean kitchen towel in a warm place until doubled in size, about 30 minutes.

Brush the top of each braid with the beaten egg and sprinkle with poppy seeds or sesame seeds. Bake for 30 to 40 minutes until golden brown.

Sopapillas

These yeasted Mexican treats are irresistible. Top them with a simple chili for a main dish, or with cinnamon and sugar or a drizzle of honey for dessert.

2 cups milk or plain soymilk

¼ cup canola oil

¼ cup warm water

¼ cup plus 1 teaspoon natural sugar

2 packages (2 tablespoons) active dry yeast

5 to 5½ cups unbleached white flour

1 teaspoon salt

Vegetable oil for frying

Scald the milk. Stir in the oil and ¼ cup sugar and set aside to cool.

Combine the water, the remaining 1 teaspoon sugar, and yeast in a bowl. Add the cooled milk and 2 cups of the flour. Beat vigorously until smooth. Cover and let rest for 10 minutes.

Add the remaining 3 to 3½ cups of flour and the salt and knead until smooth. Roll out the dough on a lightly floured surface and cut into circles about 8 inches in diameter and ⅛- to ¼-inch thick. Cover well with plastic wrap and let rise 30 minutes.

While the dough is rising, heat 1 or 2 inches of oil in a heavy-bottomed saucepan. When hot, fry the sopapillas, turning them once until golden on both sides. Remove from the oil with a slotted spoon and drain on paper towels. For the best flavor and texture, serve immediately.

Breakfast Grains and Pastries

Breakfast Grains

Breakfast Pastries

Breakfast Uppma

Uppma is a savory Indian dish made with toasted farina, more commonly known as cream of wheat. Toasting makes the wheat easier to digest. This breakfast cereal is mildly spiced—a perfect way to start the day.

1 cup cream of wheat

2 tablespoons ghee

1 teaspoon whole cumin seeds

Pinch of asafetida powder

1/2 teaspoon turmeric

1 small onion, diced

3 cups boiling water

1/4 cup minced fresh cilantro

1/2 teaspoon salt

Toast the cream of wheat in a dry skillet over medium heat until slightly browned. Stir or shake the pan frequently while toasting. Remove from the heat and set aside.

Heat the ghee in a saucepan. Add the cumin seeds and sauté until brown. Stir in the turmeric and asafetida. Add the onion and sauté until translucent. Carefully add the water and bring to a boil. Slowly whisk in the toasted cream of wheat, stirring constantly to prevent lumping. Simmer for 1 to 2 minutes, whisking continuously. Lower the heat, cover, and cook for about 10 minutes. Stir in the cilantro and salt just before serving.

Sunrise Barley Cereal

Serves 4

This spicy barley cereal will get everyone up and ready for the day. Barley flakes look like rolled oats and cook in about the same amount of time. They can be found in the bulk foods section at natural food markets. If you cannot find them, you can substitute rolled oats.

For the cereal, bring the 2 cups water to a boil in a medium saucepan and stir in the barley flakes. Lower the heat, cover, and simmer 5 to 8 minutes or until the barley is cooked.

For the masala, place the onion, coconut, chili, and ginger in a saucepan. Add the 1/2 cup water and bring to a boil. Reduce the heat, cover, and cook until the onion is tender, about 5 minutes.

While the cereal and masala are cooking, heat the ghee in a cast-iron skillet. Add the mustard seeds and fry until they pop and turn gray. Stir in the fenugreek seeds, coriander seeds, and fennel seeds and sauté until they are browned, about 3 minutes. Add the seeds to the cooked onion and mix well. Purée the masala in a blender until smooth. Stir the blended masala into the cooked barley cereal along with the salt. Mix well. Add more salt if desired.

Cereal

2 cups water

1 cup barley flakes or rolled oats

Masala

1 onion, finely chopped

1/2 cup unsweetened flaked coconut

1/2 large green chili, seeded and minced

1 1/2 teaspoons minced fresh ginger

1/2 cup water

2 teaspoons ghee

1 tablespoon whole mustard seeds

1 1/2 teaspoons whole fenugreek seeds

1 1/2 teaspoons whole coriander seeds

1/2 teaspoon whole fennel seeds

1 teaspoon salt

Oven-Roasted Fruit and Nut Granola

Serves 4 to 6

This granola keeps well in an airtight container for at least a week. Kids love it for breakfast or for a tasty snack.

4 cups rolled oats

1 cup unsweetened shredded coconut

1 cup ghee, melted, or canola oil

3/4 cup Sucanat or other natural sweetener

3/4 cup chopped nuts (almonds, walnuts, pecans)

3/4 cup raw sunflower seeds

1/4 cup sesame seeds

1 tablespoon vanilla extract

1 1/2 teaspoons ground cinnamon

3/4 teaspoon grated nutmeg

1 1/2 cups dried fruit (such as blueberries, cherries, cranberries, papaya, candied ginger, raisins, dates, or your choice)

Salt

Preheat the oven to 350°F. Combine the oats, coconut, ghee, Sucanat, nuts, seeds, vanilla extract, cinnamon, and nutmeg in a 9 x 13-inch baking dish. Mix well. Bake, stirring frequently, 30 to 40 minutes or until brown and slightly crispy.

Remove from the oven and stir in the dried fruit and salt to taste. Serve warm, or cool completely and store in a tightly covered container at room temperature.

Southern-Style Corn Grits

Corn grits are a Southern favorite. They can be served for breakfast or as a side dish at lunch or dinner. Use your favorite cheese or any combination of cheeses from pepper jack to goat cheese.

Combine the water and salt in a saucepan and bring to a boil. Whisk in the corn grits. Lower the heat, cover, and cook for 5 to 10 minutes, stirring frequently to prevent lumps and keep the grits from sticking to the bottom of the pan. When the grits have absorbed all the water and have softened, stir in the optional cheese, ghee, and pepper. Serve hot.

3 cups boiling water

1/2 teaspoon salt

1 cup yellow corn grits (commonly called polenta)

1/4 to 1/2 cup grated Monterey Jack cheese or other cheese of choice (optional)

2 teaspoons ghee

Pinch of pepper

Toasted Cream of Wheat with Cashew Butter

This simple recipe is rich, nutritious, and grounding for a good morning start.

Toast the cream of wheat in a heavy-bottomed saucepan over medium heat for 5 to 8 minutes or until lightly browned.

1 cup cream of wheat

2½ cups boiling water

½ cup raw cashew butter

1 tablespoon pure maple syrup

Pinch of salt

Slowly whisk the boiling water into the pan, beating vigorously to prevent lumps. Cover and reduce the heat to low. Cook until the water has been absorbed, about 5 minutes. Stir in the cashew butter, maple syrup, and salt and mix until well combined.

Peach Surprise Muffins

Plump, juicy Colorado peaches are abundant in the summer. These muffins are a creative way to enjoy the bounty of the season.

Preheat the oven to 375°F. Oil 12 muffin cups.

Combine the flour, baking powder, and salt in a large bowl. In a separate bowl, whisk together the milk, Sucanat, eggs, ghee, and vanilla extract. Pour into the dry ingredients and mix gently until evenly moistened.

In a third bowl, combine the peaches, optional dates, maple syrup, and cinnamon. Spoon some of the muffin batter into the prepared muffin cups, filling them only halfway. Spoon a heaping tablespoon of the peach mixture over the batter. Fill the muffin cups with the remainder of the batter and bake for 30 minutes or until browned on top.

2 cups whole wheat pastry flour

1 tablespoon baking powder

1/2 teaspoon salt

1 cup milk or buttermilk

2/3 cup Sucanat or other natural sugar

2 eggs or 1/4 cup Flaxseed Egg Replacer, page 12

6 tablespoons ghee, melted

1 teaspoon vanilla extract

2 peeled fresh peaches, cut into bite-size chunks (about 1 1/2 cups)

2 pitted dates, chopped (optional)

2 tablespoons pure maple syrup

1 teaspoon ground cinnamon

Wheat-Free Zucchini and Carob Chip Muffins

Makes 12 large muffins

Often we have guests at Shoshoni who are wheat intolerant. These muffins are a tasty alternative and can help reduce the amount of wheat-based foods in your diet.

1 cup milk or soymilk

3/4 cup ghee, melted

3/4 cup pure maple syrup or Sucanat

1/2 cup Flaxseed Egg Replacer, page 12, or 1 egg

2 cups brown rice flour

1 cup barley flour

1 tablespoon baking powder

1 teaspoon baking soda

3/4 teaspoon salt

2 cups shredded zucchini

1 cup carob chips

1/2 cup raisins or chopped pitted dates

1/2 cup (about 2 ounces) almonds, finely chopped

Preheat the oven to 350°F. Oil 12 muffin cups.

Combine the milk, ghee, maple syrup, and Flaxseed Egg Replacer in a large bowl, and beat with an electric beater on high for 1 minute.

In a separate bowl, combine the rice flour, barley flour, baking powder, baking soda, and salt. Quickly pour the wet ingredients into the flour mixture. Stir until evenly combined. Fold in the zucchini, carob chips, raisins, and almonds. Spoon into the prepared muffin cups. (These muffins don't rise very much, so fill the muffin cups as full as you like.) Bake 30 minutes or until golden brown and a toothpick inserted into the center of a muffin comes out clean.

Variation

This recipe can be enjoyed with wheat flour as well. Just substitute whole wheat pastry flour for the rice and barley flours. The muffin batter should be stiff but moist. If the batter is too thin, the muffins will not cook through properly.

Lemon Blueberry Scones

Lemon and blueberries in a classic scone are an unbeatable combination. Try these for a special breakfast or for tea.

Preheat the oven to 375°F. Lightly oil a baking sheet.

Combine the flour, 1/3 cup Sucanat, baking powder, and salt in a large bowl.

2 cups whole wheat pastry flour

1/3 cup Sucanat for baking, plus 1/2 cup Sucanat to sprinkle on scones

2 teaspoons baking powder

1/2 teaspoon salt

6 tablespoons cold ghee or unsalted butter

1 to 1 1/2 cups fresh blueberries

2 eggs, beaten

1/2 cup heavy cream

1 teaspoon natural lemon extract

1 teaspoon grated lemon zest

1/2 cup Sucanat or other natural sugar

Stir with a dry wire whisk until well blended. Cut the ghee into small pieces and work it into the flour with a pastry cutter or two forks until the largest pieces are the size of peas and the rest are well blended.

In a separate bowl, combine the eggs, cream, lemon extract, and lemon zest. Whisk until frothy.

Add the blueberries to the dry ingredients, tossing gently until they are coated with flour. Working quickly, stir the wet ingredients into the flour mixture. Mix gently until the dough forms a ball.

Turn the dough onto a lightly floured surface. Turn very gently to smooth out the dough. Roll into a square (roughly 9 x 9 inches) about 1 inch thick. Slice the dough twice vertically and twice horizontally (the dough will be cut into thirds in each direction), then cut each individual square diagonally into two triangles.

Place on the prepared baking sheet and sprinkle the tops with the 1/2 cup Sucanat. Bake 12 to 15 minutes or until the tops are golden brown.

Sesame Biscuits

Sesame seeds give these traditional biscuits extra flavor and character. Serve the biscuits Southern-style with Soy Sausage Gravy, or plain, without. Either way you'll have a quick, delicious breakfast that will keep you going strong all morning.

Preheat the oven to 375°F. Lightly oil a baking sheet.

Whisk together the flour, sesame seeds, baking powder, and salt in a medium bowl. Cut the ghee into the flour using a pastry cutter or two forks until the largest pieces are the size of peas and the rest are the consistency of bread crumbs.

Pour the milk into a large bowl. Whisk in 1/2 cup of the flour mixture, and then add the rest of the flour mixture all at once. Stir the batter gently until it is dry enough to form a ball of dough. Turn it onto a lightly floured surface and roll out into a round about 12 inches in diameter and 1 inch thick.

Use a biscuit cutter to make evenly round biscuits. Place them side by side on the prepared baking sheet so that they touch each other. Brush the tops of the biscuits with a little melted ghee and sprinkle with sesame seeds. Bake 15 to 20 minutes or until golden brown on top.

Biscuits

2 cups whole wheat pastry flour

1/4 cup white sesame seeds

2 teaspoons baking powder

1/2 teaspoon salt

3 tablespoons chilled ghee or unsalted butter

3/4 cup milk or plain soymilk

2 tablespoons ghee, melted, for topping

1 tablespoon sesame seeds, for topping

with Southern Soy Sausage Gravy

Makes about 2 to 2$\frac{1}{2}$ cups gravy

Gravy

1 tablespoon ghee

$\frac{1}{2}$ onion, minced

1 teaspoon dried sage

1 teaspoon whole fennel seeds

$\frac{1}{2}$ cup soy sausage, crumbled or diced small

$\frac{1}{4}$ cup barley flour

2 cups warm milk or plain soymilk

$\frac{1}{4}$ cup Bragg Liquid Aminos or natural soy sauce

Pinch of pepper

Heat the ghee in a cast-iron skillet. Add the onion and sauté until translucent. Stir in the sage and fennel seeds and sauté until the fennel seeds are lightly browned. Add the soy sausage and fry until brown and crispy.

Whisk in the flour, stirring constantly. When the onions are evenly coated with the flour, pour in small amounts of the warm milk, whisking constantly after each addition to create a smooth, creamy consistency. Whisk in the remaining milk, Bragg Liquid Aminos, and pepper. Simmer on medium-low for about 10 minutes or until the gravy is the thickness you desire.

Streusel Spice Buttermilk Coffee Cake

Makes 1 (9 x 13-inch) cake (about 9 servings)

This classic coffee cake is perfect for entertaining or a special family brunch.

Combine the flour, nuts, Sucanat, ghee, cinnamon, and salt in a food processor, Pulse until the mixture resembles coarse bread crumbs. Stir in the dates by hand. Set aside.

Streusel

2/3 cup whole wheat pastry flour

2/3 cup (about 3 ounces) pecans, finely chopped

2/3 cup Sucanat or other natural sugar

5 tablespoons cold ghee or unsalted butter

1 teaspoon ground cinnamon

1/4 teaspoon salt

2/3 cup chopped pitted dates

Coffee Cake

2 1/4 cups whole wheat pastry flour

1 teaspoon baking powder

1 teaspoon baking soda

1/2 teaspoon salt

1 cup Sucanat or other natural sugar

6 tablespoons chilled ghee or unsalted butter

2 eggs, or 1/4 cup Flaxseed Egg Replacer, page 12

3/4 cup buttermilk

1 teaspoon vanilla extract

Preheat the oven to 350°F. Oil a 9 x 13-inch baking pan.

Place the flour, baking powder, baking soda, and salt in a bowl and stir with a dry whisk until evenly combined. In a separate bowl, combine the Sucanat and ghee. Beat with an electric beater on high until creamed. Add the eggs and beat until well blended. Stir in the buttermilk and vanilla extract. With the electric beater on low, gradually beat in the flour mixture until smooth.

Pour half the batter into the bottom of the prepared baking pan and smooth it out with a rubber spatula. Sprinkle half the streusel evenly over the batter. Pour the remaining half of the batter evenly over the streusel and sprinkle the top evenly with the remainder of the streusel. Bake for 30 minutes or until a toothpick inserted in the center comes out clean. Cool briefly before serving.

Wheat-Free Multi-Grain Pancakes

with Fresh Blueberry Sauce

Makes 12 (4-inch) pancakes

If you are sensitive to wheat, try spelt flour. It will yield a delicious result.

Combine the flours, cornmeal, baking powder, Sucanat, baking soda, and salt in a large bowl. Gradually stir in the milk, eggs, and melted ghee. Stir very carefully. Do not beat; lumps are okay.

Heat a griddle or a cast iron skillet until hot. Add a small amount of ghee to prevent the pancakes from sticking. Ladle about 1/3 cup of batter into the pan to make a pancake about 4 inches in diameter. Cook 2 to 3 pancakes at a time, depending on the size of your pan or griddle. Cook until bubbles appear on the surface of the cake, then flip it over. Cook until golden brown, just a few minutes on each side.

Combine the blueberries, apple juice, and Sucanat in a saucepan. Bring to a boil and stir in the dissolved cornstarch. Lower the heat and simmer, stirring often, until thickened, about 5 minutes. Serve warm over the pancakes.

Pancakes

3/4 cup spelt flour or whole wheat
   pastry flour

1/4 cup oat flour

1/4 cup brown rice flour

1/4 cup cornmeal

1 tablespoon baking powder

1 tablespoon Sucanat or other natural sugar

1 teaspoon baking soda

1/2 teaspoon salt

1 1/2 cups milk, buttermilk, or plain soymilk

2 eggs, beaten, or 1/2 cup Flaxseed Egg
   Replacer, page 12

2 tablespoons melted ghee

Fresh Blueberry Sauce

1 cup fresh blueberries

1 cup unsweetened apple juice

1/4 cup Sucanat or pure maple syrup

2 tablespoons cornstarch dissolved in 2
   tablespoons cold water

Quick-Rise Cinnamon Rolls

To make the dough, combine the very warm (but not boiling) water, 2 tablespoons of the sugar, and the yeast in a small bowl. Set aside for 5 minutes for the yeast to activate.

Combine the flour, remaining sugar, baking powder, baking soda, and salt in a large bowl. Stir in the softened butter and rub it into the flour mixture with your hands to create pea-sized crumbs.

In a separate bowl, whisk together the yogurt and milk. Pour over the flour mixture. Stir to form a dough, then knead until the ingredients are well incorporated and the dough is smooth, about 5 minutes. Let rise in a warm place for about 10 minutes while you make the filling.

Dough

1/4 cup very warm water

1/2 cup natural sugar

1 package (1 tablespoon) active dry yeast

4 1/2 cups unbleached white flour or whole wheat pastry flour

2 teaspoons baking powder

1 teaspoon baking soda

1/2 teaspoon salt

1/2 cup butter, softened

1 cup plain yogurt

1/2 cup milk

We use a quick-yeasted dough that delivers delicious, hot cinnamon rolls in a short time. This old-fashioned recipe is not light on fats or sweets. One saintly Ma from Bangalore tells us, "We need to eat a little sweet on occasion, so we stay sweet."

Filling

2 sticks butter

1$\frac{1}{2}$ cups Sucanat or other natural sugar

1$\frac{1}{2}$ cups walnuts or pecans

2$\frac{1}{2}$ tablespoons ground cinnamon

$\frac{1}{2}$ cup pure maple syrup to drizzle over the top (optional)

For the filling, combine the butter, sugar, nuts, and cinnamon in a food processor and pulse to make a uniform, crumbly mixture. Reserve $\frac{1}{4}$ cup of this mixture for the crumble topping.

Preheat the oven to 375°F. Lightly oil a baking sheet. On a floured surface, roll out the dough into a large rectangle, about 12 inches (wide) by 6 inches (tall) and about $\frac{1}{4}$ inch thick. Spread the filling over the rectangle, all the way to the edges on the sides. Leave a 1-inch margin of dough on the top and bottom. Roll up the dough (like a jelly roll) from bottom to top with the filling in the center. Slice the roll into 1-inch sections with a serrated knife. Lay the slices about 1 inch apart on the prepared baking sheet with the spiral of cinnamon filling facing up. Crumble the remaining filling over the top of the rolls.

Bake for 25 to 30 minutes or until golden brown. Serve as is or drizzle the top of the hot cinnamon rolls with maple syrup.

Dairy-Free Cherry Scones

Makes about 12 scones

These egg-free drop scones are delightful and very easy to make.

Preheat the oven to 375°F. Have ready a baking sheet. Combine the 2 tablespoons Sucanat and cinnamon and set aside.

2 tablespoons Sucanat or other natural sugar

2 tablespoons ground cinnamon

2 cups whole wheat pastry flour

1/4 cup Sucanat or other natural sugar

2 teaspoons baking powder

1/2 teaspoon salt

1/4 teaspoon baking soda

3/4 cup soymilk

1/4 cup Flaxseed Egg Replacer, page 12

1/4 cup canola oil

2 cups pitted, dried sweet cherries

Combine the flour, 1/4 cup Sucanat, baking powder, salt, and baking soda in a large bowl. Stir with a dry wire whisk until evenly mixed.

In a separate bowl, combine the soymilk, Flaxseed Egg Replacer, and canola oil. Add the cherries to the flour mixture and toss gently until they are well coated with flour. Quickly stir the flaxseed mixture into the dry ingredients, blending only until the batter is evenly moistened. Do not overmix.

Drop by the spoonful onto the baking sheet and sprinkle with the reserved Sucanat and cinnamon. Bake 12 to 15 minutes or until the tops are golden brown. Best served warm.

Variation

To make wheat-free scones, substitute spelt flour for the wheat flour. Spelt flour is more water soluble than wheat flour, so make sure the batter isn't too wet. It should be moist but stiff.

Desserts

Almond Butter and Carob Chip Cookies

Makes about 24 large cookies

Almond butter is a tasty and nutritious alternative to peanut butter.

Preheat the oven to 375°F. Oil an 11 x 16 baking sheet.

Cream the butter, Sucanat, almond butter, Flaxseed Egg Replacer, and vanilla extract until smooth, by hand for about 5 minutes or with a food processor fitted with a steel blade for about 1 minute.

2 sticks unsalted butter, softened

1 cup Sucanat or other natural sugar, ground in a coffee grinder until fine

$2/3$ cup almond butter

$1/4$ cup Flaxseed Egg Replacer, page 12, or 1 egg, beaten

2 teaspoons vanilla extract

$2^{1/2}$ cups whole wheat pastry flour

$1/2$ teaspoon salt

$1/2$ cup naturally sweetened carob chips

Combine the flour and salt, and sift a little at a time into the almond butter mixture, stirring after each addition until just blended. Fold in the carob chips. The batter should be moist but stiff.

Drop by tablespoonfuls onto the prepared baking sheet. (About 12 cookies will fit per sheet.) Bake 6 to 8 minutes or until evenly browned. Cool on a wire rack.

Wheat-Free Oatmeal Raisin Cookies

Makes about 24 large cookies

You can eat these naturally delicious cookies without feeling guilty. Kids love them for a healthy snack in their lunchbox or anytime.

2 cups spelt flour

3/4 teaspoon baking soda

3/4 teaspoon baking powder

1/2 teaspoon salt

1/2 teaspoon ground cinnamon

1/2 teaspoon grated nutmeg

1 1/2 cups Sucanat or other natural sugar

1 stick unsalted butter, softened, or 1/2 cup canola oil

1 cup unsweetened apple juice

2 eggs, beaten, or 1/4 cup Flaxseed Egg Replacer, page 12

2 1/2 teaspoons vanilla extract

3 1/2 cups rolled oats

1 cup raisins

1 cup walnuts, coarsely chopped

Preheat oven to 350°F. Lightly oil a baking sheet.

Combine the flour, baking soda, baking powder, salt, cinnamon, and nutmeg in a large bowl. In a separate bowl, combine the Sucanat and softened butter and blend until creamy. Stir in the apple juice, eggs, and vanilla extract and blend again briefly.

Stir the dry ingredients into the butter mixture, a little at a time, until well blended and smooth. Fold in the oats, raisins, and walnuts.

Drop the dough by heaping tablespoonfuls onto the prepared baking sheet and lightly press the cookies with the palm of your hand. About 12 cookies will fit per sheet. Bake for 8 to 10 minutes or until golden brown. Cool on a wire rack.

Chewy Cherry Granola Bars

This is another delicious, nutritious snack for kids. Wrap the bars individually to keep them fresh.

1³/4 cups whole wheat pastry flour

³/4 teaspoon baking soda

³/4 teaspoon baking powder

¹/2 teaspoon salt

¹/2 teaspoon ground cinnamon

1³/4 cups Sucanat

2 sticks unsalted butter, softened

¹/2 cup frozen apple juice concentrate, thawed

2¹/2 teaspoons vanilla extract

3 cups rolled oats

2 cups dried sweet cherries

1 cup pecans, coarsely chopped

Preheat the oven to 350°F. Combine the flour, baking soda, baking powder, salt, and cinnamon in a bowl. Stir with a dry whisk until evenly combined.

In a separate large bowl, using an electric beater on medium speed, beat together the Sucanat, butter, apple juice concentrate, and vanilla extract. Stir the flour mixture into the butter mixture and blend until smooth. Stir in the rolled oats, cherries, and pecans.

Press the batter into an 11 x 16-inch jelly roll pan and bake 15 to 20 minutes. Let cool in the pan. When cool, cut into rectangular bars.

Anise Pizzelles with Strawberry Cream

These Italian waffle cookies were inspired by Faith's Italian mother-in-law, Ella Putorti.

Beat the eggs, adding the sugar gradually. Beat until the mixture is smooth. Stir in the cooled melted butter, anise seeds, and vanilla extract and mix well. In a separate bowl, sift together the flour and baking powder. Gradually add the flour to the egg mixture. Stir until evenly combined. The dough should be sticky enough to be dropped by spoonfuls.

Cookie Dough

6 eggs

1½ cups natural sugar

1 cup butter, melted and cooled

2 tablespoons whole anise seeds

1 teaspoon vanilla extract

3½ cups unbleached white or whole wheat pastry flour

3 teaspoons baking powder

Strawberry Cream

2 cups heavy whipping cream

2 tablespoons natural sugar

½ teaspoon vanilla extract

½ pint fresh strawberries

Heat a pizzelle iron (Italian waffle cookie maker) until hot. Place a generous tablespoon of the cookie batter in the center of the waffle mold and press the mold together. Cook the pizzelles for about 1 minute or until the cookies are nicely browned. Remove the cookies and lay them flat or roll them into a cone shape to be stuffed with strawberries and whipped cream, chocolate mousse, or other fillings.

Slice the strawberries and sprinkle them with sugar. Let the berries sit for 10 minutes to release their juice. Whip the cream with a wire whip, electric beater, or food processor until it holds firm peaks. Fold the berries and their juice into the whipped cream. Fit a pastry bag with a plain tube. Fill the pastry bag with the Strawberry Cream and pipe the mixture into curled pizzelles or fill the curled pizzelles using a spoon.

Fresh Ginger Cake

Makes 1 bundt cake (about 6 to 8 servings)

This cake is infused with the spicy taste of fresh ginger. Lemon gives the finishing touch.

Preheat the oven to 350°F. Grease and flour a bundt cake pan.

Combine the flour, baking powder, and salt in a medium bowl. In a separate large bowl, whisk together the Sucanat, molasses, eggs, milk, and ginger. Whisk in the melted butter. Stir in the dry ingredients, mixing only until smooth. Scrape the batter into the prepared cake pan. Bake for 35 to 40 minutes or until a toothpick inserted into the center of the cake comes out clean.

Bundt Cake

3 cups whole wheat pastry flour

2 teaspoons baking powder

1/2 teaspoon salt

1 cup Sucanat or other natural sugar

1 cup blackstrap molasses

2 eggs, beaten, or 1/2 cup Flaxseed Egg Replacer, page 12

1/2 cup milk or plain soymilk

1/2 cup minced fresh ginger

1 1/2 cups ghee or unsalted butter, melted

with Lemon Almond Glaze

Drain the almonds and place them in a blender. Add the milk and process until very smooth. Transfer to a bowl.

Lemon Almond Glaze

1 cup blanched almonds, soaked overnight in water to cover

1 cup milk or plain soymilk

1 cup natural sugar

1/4 cup unsalted butter, melted

Juice of 1 large lemon (about 1/4 cup)

1 tablespoon grated lemon zest

Pinch of salt

Coarsely chopped toasted almonds, for garnish (optional)

For a finer glaze, blend the natural sugar in a coffee grinder until it is a fine powder. Stir into the almond paste along with the melted butter, lemon juice, lemon zest, and salt. Refrigerate for about 1 hour in order for the glaze to firm. Drizzle the glaze over the bundt cake. Garnish with a sprinkle of coarsely chopped toasted almonds, if desired.

Autumn Fresh Apple Spice Cake

Autumn is the season for crisp juicy apples. Use this delicious recipe for a quick cake that is spicy and moist.

P reheat the oven to 350°F. Oil and flour an 8 x 8-inch baking pan.

Combine the flour, sugar, baking soda, cinnamon, cloves, nutmeg, and salt in a large bowl. Whisk until evenly combined. Add the buttermilk, melted ghee, and almond and vanilla extracts, and stir until just mixed. Fold in the chopped apple and almonds.

Pour into the prepared baking pan and spread evenly with a rubber spatula. Bake 40 to 45 minutes. Let cool before removing from the pan.

1 1/2 cups whole wheat pastry flour

1 cup Sucanat or other natural sugar

1 teaspoon baking soda

1 teaspoon ground cinnamon

1/2 teaspoon ground cloves

1/2 teaspoon grated nutmeg

1/2 teaspoon salt

1 cup buttermilk

1/2 cup ghee, melted

1 tablespoon almond extract

1 teaspoon vanilla extract

1 Granny Smith or your favorite kind of apple, peeled and coarsely chopped (about 1 cup)

1/2 cup (about 2 ounces) blanched almonds, coarsely chopped

Chocolate "Cream" Pie with Whole Wheat Graham Crust

This pie is an instant hit in summer. The guests and residents at Shoshoni can't tell it's non-dairy. For diehard chocolate lovers, use semi-sweet chocolate chips, or for a rich, delicious alternative, try using naturally-sweetened carob chips.

Preheat the oven to 350°F. Crumble the graham crackers into the work bowl of a food processor. Add the melted butter and pulse to mix well. Press into a 9-inch pie pan and bake for 10 minutes to lightly toast. Cool.

Graham Cracker Crust

2 packages natural, whole wheat graham crackers (about 4 cups crumbled)

3/4 cup unsalted butter, melted

Cream Pie

3 cups carob chips or semi-sweet chocolate chips

1/4 cup ghee or unsalted butter, melted

2 (12-ounce) packages extra-firm silken tofu

1 cup powdered natural sugar

1 tablespoon fresh lemon juice

1/4 teaspoon grated nutmeg

Pinch of salt

Combine the chocolate chips and ghee in a heavy-bottomed saucepan. Place over low heat until melted. Remove from the heat and cool for 5 minutes.

Place the tofu in a food processor and add the melted chips and ghee, powdered sugar, lemon juice, nutmeg, and salt. Blend until very creamy, like pudding. Spoon into the graham cracker crust and chill for at least 2 hours. The pie will be firmer and slice better if it is chilled several hours or overnight.

Variation

This pie also bakes well and will turn out similar to cheesecake. Follow the directions for the basic cream pie, then bake the pie in a preheated 350°F oven for 30 minutes or until set in the middle. Let chill at least 3 hours or overnight before serving.

Gateau a l'Orange

Faith taught this recipe at the Ouray Culinary Arts Festival featuring Colorado's top chefs. This is a moist and elegant special-occasion cake.

Cake

6 eggs, room temperature

1 cup natural sugar

1 cup plus 2 tablespoons
  unbleached white flour

2 tablespoons canola oil

Filling

1 cup natural sugar

$1/2$ cup water

6 egg yolks

1 pound unsalted butter, softened

$1/2$ cup fresh orange juice

Garnish

$1/4$ cup fresh orange juice

1 cup orange marmalade

1 cup toasted sliced almonds

Preheat the oven to 350°F. Butter and lightly dust an 8-inch round cake pan with flour.

Using an electric beater, whip the eggs and sugar in a large bowl until light in color and tripled in volume. Sift the flour over the surface of the beaten eggs and sugar, then fold it in with a rubber spatula. When all the flour is incorporated, fold in the oil.

Pour the batter into the prepared cake pan. Bake for 30 minutes or until a toothpick inserted in the center comes out clean. Cool for 5 minutes in the pan, then remove from the pan and cool completely.

To make the filling, combine the sugar and water in a saucepan and bring to a boil. Boil for 5 minutes. Place the egg yolks in a bowl and pour the hot sugar syrup over them. Using an electric beater, immediately whip at high speed until quadrupled in volume and very light and fluffy.

When the mixture has cooled to room temperature, turn the beater speed to low and gradually beat in the softened butter 1 tablespoon at a time, alternating with the $\frac{1}{2}$ cup orange juice. When all the butter and juice have been added, turn up the speed to medium and whip until smooth and fluffy.

Split the cake in three horizontal layers using a serrated knife. Drizzle the $\frac{1}{4}$ cup orange juice evenly over each layer of cake. Spread one-third of the filling between the layers and frost the sides and top of the cake with the remaining filling.

Freeze the cake for 30 to 60 minutes to set the filling. Remove from the freezer and carefully spread the top and sides of the cake with a thin layer of marmalade. Press the toasted sliced almonds into the sides. Refrigerate until serving time.

Rudi's Marjolaine Cake

Faith created this hazelnut, almond, and chocolate cake for the Art Fest Tournament when she was the award-winning chef and owner of Rudi's Restaurant in Boulder, Colorado. It won first place! She has been making it ever since for special occasions.

Preheat the oven to 350°F. Place the almonds on a dry baking sheet and the hazelnuts on another dry baking sheet. Toast the nuts separately in the oven until light brown, about 10 minutes. Cool. Rub the hazelnuts together between your hands to remove their skins. Grind the nuts together in a nut grinder or food processor until they have the consistency of coarse flour.

Cake

2 cups (8 ounces) blanched whole almonds

1 cup (5 ounces) hazelnuts

1 cup natural sugar

1/4 cup unbleached white flour

8 egg whites at room temperature

Combine the ground nuts with the sugar and flour. Beat the egg whites until stiff but not dry. Gently fold in the nut mixture. Butter a 10-inch round cake pan and dust with flour to prevent sticking. Spread the cake batter evenly in the pan and bake for 40 to 45 minutes. The cake should solidify and dry out but it will not brown very much.

After baking, let the cake sit in the pan for 5 minutes. Remove, set onto a cake rack, and cool.

Slice the cake horizontally in two or three layers using a serrated knife. Spread Chocolate Soufflé (recipe follows) between each layer and on the top and sides of the cake. Chill or freeze until the Chocolate Soufflé hardens.

Note: The cake may be prepared several days to a week in advance and frozen.

Crowned with Raspberry Mousse

Chocolate Soufflé

8 ounces bittersweet chocolate

1 cup heavy cream

1 ounce Grand Marnier (optional)

Fresh Raspberry Mousse

1 pint fresh raspberries, washed

Juice and grated zest of 1 lemon (about 3 tablespoons juice and 2 to 3 teaspoons zest)

1/2 cup natural sugar

3 egg whites

1 cup cream

1 teaspoon (1 envelope) vegetable gelatin (see note below)

Melt the chocolate in the top of a double boiler. Stir in the cream and optional liqueur. Transfer the mixture to a bowl and chill 15 to 20 minutes or until fairly thick but not hard. Beat with an electric mixer until light and fluffy. Best used within several hours of being made.

Butter a 9-inch ring mold and set aside.

Place the raspberries in a bowl with the lemon juice and zest. Sprinkle the sugar over the berries and let them sit for 15 minutes or until very juicy. Drain the juice from the berries into a saucepan and add the gelatin. Bring to a boil, stirring constantly to ensure the gelatin is well dissolved. Stir back into the berries.

Using an electric beater, whip the egg whites until firm but not dry. Gradually fold into the raspberries adding about 1/3 at a time. Chill about 30 minutes or until firm enough that during stirring the juice doesn't sink to the bottom of the bowl. Whip the cream and gently fold it into the mousse.

Spoon the mousse into the prepared ring mold and chill for several hours or overnight. You'll have some extra mousse. It can be put into a decorative mold or bowl and chilled until firm.

Note: Using 1 teaspoon of vegetable gelatin will make a very delicate, fragile mousse. For your first attempt, you may want to double the amount of gelatin, as unmolding the mousse can be a tricky procedure.

recipe continues on next page

Rudi's Marjolaine Cake (cont'd)

Chocolate Sauce

2 ounces bittersweet chocolate

1/2 cup milk

1 ounce Grand Marnier (optional)

Final Assembly

The chilled Marjolaine cake

Fresh raspberry mousse in ring mold

2 cups whipping cream

1/4 cup natural sugar

1 kiwi fruit, peeled and sliced in 8 circles

1/2 cup fresh raspberries, for garnish

1/2 cup fresh strawberries, sliced in half, for garnish

1 cup Chocolate Sauce (see recipe above; optional)

Pastry bag with start tip (optional)

Melt the chocolate in the top of a double boiler. Stir in the milk and optional Grand Marnier.

Using an electric mixer, whip the cream and sugar until it forms soft peaks and is firm but not too stiff.

Place the Marjolaine cake on a decorative tray or silver platter. Run a knife around the edge of the mousse ring (briefly dip the mold in a little warm water if the mousse seems to be stuck), unmold the mousse directly onto a flat, buttered plate, then slide it onto the Marjolaine cake.

Fill the center of the ring with the whipped cream. If desired, pipe a decorative border of whipped cream onto the side using a pastry bag. Make a ring of kiwi fruit and berries around the whipped cream in the center of the cake.

As the colors are vivid and presentation impressive, let your guests see the cake whole, making it a feast for the eyes. While serving, drizzle a little chocolate sauce over each slice. The cake may be assembled several hours before being served and kept well chilled.

Basic Pastry Crust

Makes 1 (9-inch) crust (serves 6 to 8)

Use this flaky crust for all of our pie recipes.

2 cups whole wheat pastry flour

1/2 teaspoon salt

1 cup unsalted butter, cold

1/2 cup ice cold water

Combine the flour and salt in a medium bowl. Cut in the butter using a pastry cutter or two forks until the flour is the texture of cornmeal. Stir in the water and quickly form the dough into a ball. Cover with plastic wrap and refrigerate for 30 minutes.

Dust the countertop with a little flour. Using a rolling pin, roll the chilled dough into a circle about 10 inches in diameter. Lightly oil a 9-inch pie pan with a teaspoon of butter or canola oil. This helps the crust to brown on the bottom as the pie bakes. Roll the dough circle around the rolling pin and then gently unroll it into the pie pan and press against the sides and bottom.

Toasting the crust

Many of our recipes call for toasting the crust prior to filling it. This prevents the bottom of the crust from staying too moist while the edges brown. You can do this by placing 1 cup of dry beans into the crust and baking it in a preheated 350°F oven for 5 to 10 minutes. The dry beans keep the bottom of the crust from bubbling up (the beans can be discarded after the crust has cooled).

Fresh Strawberry Pie

This no-bake pie is fast, easy, and fresh. It is a perfect way to enjoy the abundance of sweet strawberries in springtime.

Preheat the oven to 375°F. Prepare the pastry crust as directed and bake it for 10 minutes or until golden brown. Cool.

5 cups whole fresh strawberries

1 cup granulated fructose or natural sugar

3 tablespoons cornstarch

1/4 teaspoon salt

2 cups water

1 tablespoon fresh lemon juice

1 Basic Pastry Crust, page 229, or your favorite recipe

Clean, stem, and drain the strawberries well. Arrange about 3 cups of whole berries over the bottom of the cooled crust. With a fork, crush the remaining berries in a saucepan. Stir in the fructose, cornstarch, and salt and heat, stirring often, until the mixture comes to a boil and thickens. Lower the heat and let the mixture simmer for 1 minute longer. Remove from the heat, stir in the lemon juice, and allow the mixture to cool.

Spoon the sauce over the berries in the pie crust. Chill until the glaze is set. Serve with whipped cream, if desired.

Cranberry Squash Pie

Makes 1 (9-inch) pie (serves 6 to 8)

Here is a delightful alternative to pumpkin pie.

Preheat the oven to 350°F. Toast the crust for 5 minutes according to the directions on page 229. Cool the crust and discard the beans.

1 (9-inch) pie crust (use our Basic Pastry Crust, page 229, or your favorite recipe)

2 cups cooked and mashed butternut or acorn squash

3 eggs, beaten

1/2 cup fresh cranberries, coarsely chopped

1/2 cup fresh orange juice

1/2 cup sour cream

1/2 cup natural sugar

Pinch of salt

Combine the squash, eggs, cranberries, orange juice, sour cream, sugar, and salt in a large bowl. Mix well and pour into the cooled pie crust. Bake for 45 to 60 minutes or until set. Serve warm or chilled.

Southern Pecan Pie

Makes 1 (9-inch) pie (serves 6 to 8)

This popular holiday pie tastes even better with natural sugar and pure maple syrup.

Preheat the oven to 350°F. Toast the crust for 5 minutes according to the directions on page 229. Cool the crust and discard the beans.

1 (9-inch) pie crust (use our Basic Pastry Crust, page 229, or your favorite recipe)

1 cup natural brown sugar

1 stick (1/4 pound) butter, melted

3 eggs, beaten

1/2 cup pure maple syrup

1 teaspoon vanilla extract

1/2 teaspoon salt

1 1/4 cups pecan halves

Combine the sugar and butter in a large bowl. Using an electric beater, add the eggs and beat until smooth. Add the maple syrup, vanilla extract, and salt, and beat until smooth. Stir in the pecan halves.

Pour into the cooled pie crust and bake for 45 minutes or until set. Remove from the oven and cool at least 1 hour before serving.

Classic Saffron and Pistachio Rice Pudding

This rich favorite is a classic to top off a special Indian feast.

Rinse the rice in a colander until the rinse water is clear. Combine the milk and saffron in a saucepan and bring to a boil. Stir in the rice and fructose. Simmer uncovered on very low heat for 30 minutes or until the rice is soft and the pudding has reduced to a creamy consistency. Stir in the chopped pistachios and cardamom. Serve warm or chilled.

3/4 cup white basmati rice

5 1/2 cups milk

1/8 teaspoon saffron threads

1/2 cup granulated fructose or natural sugar

1/2 cup shelled pistachios, finely chopped

1/4 teaspoon ground cardamom

Baked Bananas
with Toasted Almonds and Maple Syrup

Serves 6

Try these mouth-watering bananas with a scoop of vanilla ice cream for a special occasion treat.

1 tablespoon canola oil or softened butter

6 ripe bananas, peeled and cut in half lengthwise

3 ounces low-fat cream cheese

Pinch of grated nutmeg

1/4 cup pure maple syrup (optional)

2 tablespoons sliced almonds, toasted

Preheat the oven to 400°F. Lightly coat an 8 x 12 glass baking dish with the oil. Arrange the bananas in the baking dish cut side up. Top with dots (about 1 tablespoon per banana) of cream cheese and sprinkle with a pinch of nutmeg. Bake for about 15 minutes or until the bananas are tender and the cream cheese bubbles. Drizzle with the optional maple syrup, if desired, and sprinkle with the toasted almonds.

Cardamom Poached Pears

Serves 6

These warm, spiced pears make an elegant, easy dessert.

Place 3 cups of water in a saucepan that is large enough for all the pears to sit upright. Add the cinnamon and cardamom and bring to a boil.

6 fresh pears, peeled and cored (remove the cores with an apple corer)

6 cardamom pods (break open, remove the outer shell, and collect the black seeds)

3 cinnamon sticks, broken in half

2 tablespoons pure maple syrup (optional)

Remove from the heat and place the pears in the pot, bottoms down. Reduce the heat to low and return the pot to the heat. Cover and simmer the pears until they are tender but not mushy, about 10 minutes.

Transfer the pears to individual dessert dishes and add a few spoonfuls of the sweet cooking broth to each dish. Drizzle the pears with maple syrup, if desired. Serve warm.

Date Soufflé

This dish is fast, elegant, and delicious.

If using a fresh pineapple, remove the top, bottom, and thick skin using a sharp knife. Cut the fruit away from the hard center core, chop it into small chunks, and place it in a bowl. Using your hands or a wooden spoon, coarsely mash the chunks so the mixture is a little juicy.

Whip the cream with a wire whip, electric beater, or food processor until it holds firm peaks. Cream the cheese with an electric mixer, beating in the bananas, maple syrup, and lemon juice. Stir in the pineapple, dates, and pecans. Fold in the whipped cream. Fill custard or dessert cups and freeze 20 minutes or refrigerate several hours.

1 fresh pineapple, or 2 cups crushed canned pineapple, lightly drained

1 cup heavy whipping cream

8 ounces cream cheese, softened

3 ripe bananas, mashed

1/4 cup pure maple syrup

1 tablespoon fresh lemon juice

1/2 cup chopped dates

1/2 cup chopped pecans

Fresh Almond-Stuffed Figs in Yogurt

Shanti's grandmother had a fig tree in her backyard. Remembering how delicious and sweet the figs were straight from the tree, she created this easy dessert. It's great for brunch or a light luncheon.

Press one whole almond into each fig. Set the figs side by side in a shallow dish. Pour the apple juice over them and let marinate for at least 1 hour in the refrigerator. Drain and reserve the juice.

Combine the yogurt, honey, and the juice from marinating. Pour into six chilled champagne or dessert glasses and top each portion with two stuffed figs.

12 fresh figs, peeled

12 whole blanched almonds

1/2 cup unsweetened apple juice

1/2 cup plain yogurt

2 teaspoons honey

Gulab Jamun

These traditional Indian fried milk dumplings in a sweet, rose-scented syrup are absolutely irresistible.

Combine the dry milk, flour, and baking soda in a large bowl. Mix well. Gradually work in the 6 tablespoons of ghee, adding 3 tablespoons at a time.

2 cups nonfat dry milk

1/2 cup unbleached white flour

1/4 teaspoon baking soda

6 tablespoons melted ghee at room temperature

6 to 8 tablespoons milk

6 cups water

2 cups natural sugar

7 cardamom pods

2 cups ghee or vegetable oil for deep-frying

2 teaspoons rosewater or orange blossom water

Using both hands, rub the mixture between your palms so that the ghee is evenly distributed. Stir in the milk and mix well to make a stiff dough.

Knead the dough directly in the bowl until the dough comes together in a ball, about 5 minutes. If it is not moist enough, add a little water, about 1 tablespoon at a time, until the dough comes together in a ball. Remove from the bowl and knead for 5 minutes longer.

Break off 1 tablespoon of the dough and roll it between your palms to make a ball. If the dough sticks to your hands and crumbles, rub some melted ghee over your palms. Place the gulab jamun balls on a sheet of waxed paper on a dry baking sheet. Continue forming the balls until all the dough is used then set aside.

Combine the water and sugar in a saucepan. Bring to a boil, reduce the heat, and simmer for 30 minutes. Open the cardamom pods, crush the small black seeds inside, and add to the simmering syrup. Cook 10 minutes longer.

Heat the 2 cups ghee or vegetable oil in a wok or saucepan. Fry the balls a few at a time until browned on all sides. Drain on paper towels. When all the balls are fried, bring the syrup back to a boil, then lower the heat. Add the rosewater and all the fried balls. Cook for 10 to 15 minutes or until the balls swell up and float. Remove the balls from the syrup with a slotted spoon and place in a large bowl. Serve 3 or 4 balls per person in a bowl with a ladle of syrup.

Note: We have served this dish both warm and cold. It is delicious either way. However, it is more traditionally served warm or at room temperature. When chilled, serve 3 or 4 balls per person topped with a ladle of syrup. When storing leftover gulab jamun in the refrigerator, put them in a little bit of the syrup so they don't become hard, but don't use too much syrup or they can become soggy.

Menu Ideas

Vegetarian food offers an endless amount of possibilities when putting together a menu. Here are sample holiday menus that we use at Shoshoni, plus sample daily menus for one week. We always try to have a minimum of four dishes at a meal, but for a simple dinner at home, two dishes may be plenty. Try preparing more for special occasions or for entertaining.

Fresh Herb and Baby Greens Salad, page 30

Cream of Asparagus Soup, page 87

Warm Beet and Carrot Salad
with Fresh Mint, page 44

Acorn Squash Baked in
Cashew Sauce, page 126

Shiitake Mushrooms Stuffed with Wild Rice
on a Bed of Greens, page 134

Southern Pecan Pie, page 232

Baked Corn and Coconut Kachoris, page 20

Spicy Plum Chutney, page 57

Cucumber Mint Raita, page 60

Gingered Chickpeas with Louki Squash
and Roasted Red Peppers, page 102

Tender Cauliflower in Spiced
Cottage Cheese Sauce, page 162

Indian Fried Rice with Pistachios, Fresh
Spinach, and Tofu, page 171

Gulab Jamun, page 238

Millet Croquettes with Coriander
Spiced Yogurt, page 24

Tossed Greens and Strawberry Salad, page 38

Champignons Eleganté, page 130

Pumpkin and Lentil Soup with
Fresh Fennel, page 98

Artichokes Florentine, page 128

Fresh Ginger Cake with Lemon
Almond Glaze, page 220

Asparagus Kofta with Curried
Cottage Cheese Sauce, page 18

Golden Mung Dal Sambar with
Coconut Milk, page 79

Curried Zucchini and Bell Peppers with Fresh
Country-Style Panir Cheese, page 106

Fragrant Basmati Rice With Cashews, page 166

Holiday Cranberry Walnut Chutney, page 56

Mixed Greens with Toasted Coconut
and Hot Chilies, page 152

Cardamom Poached Pears, page 235

Here is a week of sample menus that reflect what we serve daily at Shoshoni. Please note that we serve our big meal of the day at lunchtime, following the Aryuvedic ideal of eating lighter in the evening.

Monday

Breakfast

Breakfast Uppma, page 200
Dairy-Free Cherry Scones, page 214
Fresh fruit

Lunch

Warm Beet and Carrot Salad
with Fresh Mint, page 44
Fresh Spinach and Basil Pesto Stuffed Shells
with Savory Red Sauce, page 108
Fresh Italian Herb and Roasted
Garlic Focaccia, page 190
Almond Butter and Carob Chip
Cookies, page 216

Dinner

Cajun-Style Louisiana Gumbo, page 85
Southern-Style Quinoa Pilaf, page 174
Steamed Kale with Sliced Dates
and Toasted Pecans, page 161
Fresh bread

Tuesday

Breakfast

Oven Roasted Fruit and Nut
Granola, page 202
Fresh fruit and yogurt
Peach Surprise Muffins, page 205

Lunch

Cucumber Mint Raita, page 60
Matar Panir (green peas with homemade
cheese), page 114
Bulgur Pilaf, page 167
Ginger Potato Curry, page 147
Golden Mung Dal Sambar with
Coconut Milk, page 79

Dinner

Seasonal Khichari
(see pages 177 through 181)
Fresh Herb and Baby Greens Salad, page 30,
with Yogurt Parmesan Dressing, page 51
Whole Grain Challah, page 196
Date Soufflé, page 236

Wednesday

Breakfast

Sunrise Barley Cereal, page 201
Streusel Spice Buttermilk Coffee Cake,
page 210
Fresh fruit and yogurt

Lunch

Mediterranean Red Lentil and Spinach Stew
with Currants, page 91
Toasted Millet Tabouli Salad, page 37
Summer Squash and Grilled Bell Pepper Torte
with Ricotta Cheese, page 120

Dinner

Golden Baked Curry Potatoes, page 149
Young Japanese Eggplant and Cauliflower
Curry, page 163
Indian Fried Rice with Pistachios, Fresh
Spinach, and Tofu, page 171
Cardamom Poached Pears, page 235

Thursday

Breakfast

Wheat-free Multigrain Pancakes with
Blueberry Sauce, page 211
Fresh fruit and yogurt

Lunch

Trés Colores Vegetable Salad, page 40
Fajitas with Pan-Fried Tempeh in Chipotle
Lime Marinade, page 138
Toasted Almond and Chili Pepper Rice,
page 175
Refried beans
Zesty Mango Salsa, page 64
Sopapillas, page 198

Dinner

Fresh Herb and Baby Greens Salad, page 30,
with Fresh Mint and Carrot Dressing, page 49
Mountain Yogi Khichari, page 179
Sweet Potato Biscuits, page 193

Sunday

Breakfast

Southern-Style Corn Grits, page 203
Quick-Rise Cinnamon Rolls, page 212
Fresh fruit
Yogurt

Dinner

Herbed Vegetable Barley Soup, page 90
Wilted Spinach and Feta Salad, page 42
Whole Grain Challah Bread, page 196

Friday

Breakfast

Toasted Cream of Wheat
with Cashew Butter, page 204
Lemon Blueberry Scones, page 207
Fresh fruit

Lunch

Thai Rice Noodle and Peanut Salad, page 36
Thai Vegetable Curry with Tofu, page 94
Fragrant Basmati Rice, page 166
Wheat-Free Oatmeal Raisin Cookies, page 217

Dinner

Cream of Broccoli and Cashew Soup, page 88
Feta Rolled Eggplant, page 21
Shiitake Mushrooms Stuffed with Wild Rice
on a Bed of Greens, page 134
Italian Zucchini Pancakes, page 111
Chocolate "Cream" Pie with Whole Wheat
Graham Cracker Crust, page 223

Saturday

Breakfast

Sesame Biscuits with Southern
Soy Sausage Gravy, page 208
Fruit and tea

Lunch

Vegetarian Caesar Salad, page 41
Lasagne Primavera with Whole Wheat
Noodles, page 112
Oven-Roasted Green Beans
with Fresh Basil, page 150
Fresh Ginger Cake with Lemon Almond
Glaze, page 220

Dinner

Sesame Snow Pea Salad, page 33
Tomato Flan, page 123
Baked Potatoes in Cashew Sauce
with Fresh Chives, page 144
Autumn Fresh Apple Spice Cake, page 222

Sunday Lunch

(On Sundays we serve an Indian vegetarian feast. The dishes vary week to week.)

Fresh Coconut and Green Chili Chutney,
page 54
Fresh Ginger and Date Chutney, page 55
Warming Whole Mung Dal with Winter
Squash, page 81
Fennel, Raisin, and Walnut Rice, page 170

Potato Tikkis Stuffed with Green Peas,
page 154
Saag Panir, page 115
Baked Corn and Coconut Kachoris, page 20
Yogurt
Gulab Jamun, page 238
Chai (spiced tea)

Shoshoni Yoga Retreat offers healing for body, mind, and spirit.

Shoshoni Health Therapies

People come to Shoshoni for the relaxing atmosphere, meditation classes, hatha yoga, and health therapies. Shoshoni offers nurturing massage, facials, and traditional Ayurvedic health therapies to relax the body, mind, and spirit.

As a guest at Shoshoni, you have the opportunity to enjoy individual health therapies or rejuvenation packages over a weekend or week.

Rejuvenation Retreat (2 nights)

Holiday Rejuvenation Retreat (3 nights)

3-Day Siddha-Vaidya Retreat

7-Day Siddha-Vaidya Retreat

Day Retreat

Siddha-Vaidya

Siddha-Vaidya ("knowledge of health") treatments stem from the Ayurvedic tradition, India's ancient and powerful healing science. Working with the body's own healing mechanism, Ayurvedic health therapies nourish the body and spirit, and initiate a profound healing process on all levels. They relax, detoxify, and rejuvenate the body from the inside out. Unique to this tradition, these treatments promote healing, and naturally encourage a meditative state.

Shoshoni Yoga Retreat ~ PO Box 410 ~ Rollinsville, CO 80474
(303) 642-0116 ~ info@shoshoni.org
www.shoshoni.org

Index

Yoga Kitchen

BOOK PUBLISHING COMPANY

since 1974—books that educate, inspire, and empower

To find your favorite vegetarian and soyfood products online, visit:

www.healthy-eating.com

More Fabulous Beans
Barb Bloomfield
1-57067-146-X $14.95

Coconut Oil for Health and Beauty
Cynthia Holzapfel
Laura Holzapfel
1-57067-158-3 $9.95

Angel Foods
Healthy Recipes for Heavenly Bodies
Cherie Soria
1-57067-156-7 $19.95

Simple Treats
Ellen Abraham
1-57067-137-0 $12.95

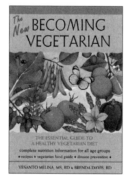

The New Becoming Vegetarian
Vesanto Melina, R.D.,
Brenda Davis, R.D.,
1-57067-144-3 $19.95

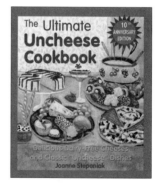

The Ultimate Uncheese Cookbook
Joanne Stepaniak
1-57067-151-6 $15.95

Purchase these health titles and cookbooks from your local bookstore or
natural food store, or you can buy them directly from:

Book Publishing Company • P.O. Box 99 • Summertown, TN 38483
1-800-695-2241

Please include $3.95 per book for shipping and handling.